Every Kid A Winner:

Accountability in Education

Every Kid A Winner:

Accountability in Education

by
Leon M. Lessinger

**Former U.S. Associate Commissioner of Education
and Callaway Professor of Education at Georgia State University**

Simon and Schuster • New York

Library of Congress Catalog Card Number: 76–135652
SBN671–20800–4
This edition is published by arrangement
with Science Research Associates, Inc.

Foreword

We are all managers of precious and limited resources: a planet stocked with life and beauty and opportunity beyond telling; a heritage of freedom as Americans bought so dearly in the sacrifice and work and enterprise of those who went before us. In the 1970s we shall account for that stewardship. It does not take prophetic vision to know that we shall all discover the very real connection between the lives we lead, the careers we pursue, the institutions we support, the thoughts we think, the values we hold, the priorities we attack, and our future as a people.

The first exercise in accountability might center on the care and nurture of our children. We are stewards of their education and training and the education system we have created consists of more than the schools. Over the years we have gradually dispatched more and more of our personal responsibilities for the young to paid and professional strangers. The good and bad results of our stewardship are coming home for all to see.

Leon M. Lessinger
August 6, 1970

Contents

Design by
Judith Olson

Calligraphy by
Chad Michel

Acknowledgements

We wish to acknowledge the following for permission to reprint material:

Daniel P. Moynihan, "Toward a National Urban Policy," © National Affairs, Inc., 1969.

Educational Technology magazine for "Performance Contracting as Catalyst for Reform," editor's note, August 1969 issue; and Allen Calvin, "Let's Reward Good Teachers," October 1969 issue.

"Accountability," an editorial, from *Instructor*, R. Pratt Krull, Jr., Editor, © Instructor Publications, Inc.

Edward C. Banfield, "The Political Implications of Metropolitan Growth," reprinted by permission from *Daedalus*, Journal of the American Academy of Arts and Sciences, Boston, Massachusetts, Volume 90, Number 1.

Introduction

Introduction

Faced with new problems, American schools are seeking new means for solving them. Leon Lessinger demonstrated while Superintendent of Schools in San Mateo, California, that a new system could be designed that resulted in greatly increased educational effectiveness. This involved new patterns of administration, the use of different incentives for the school staff to test promising innovations, and the employment of appropriate appraisal procedures to discover what actually worked.

Later, as U.S. Associate Commissioner for Elementary and Secondary Education, he was able to observe problems in schools throughout the nation and to encourage development of the principles he found effective in San Mateo. His stimulation was largely responsible for the revolutionary approach instituted in Texarkana for teaching disadvantaged children. The move from Washington to a professorship in Georgia enabled Lessinger to write a brief but comprehensive statement of the concepts basic to this fundamental approach to educational improvement.

This volume is a clear formulation of the thinking behind the development of what he calls "educational engineering." He also outlines in some detail the steps schools can follow in taking the initiative in attacking their difficult educational problems. He explains how these procedures are likely not only to find more efficient solutions but also to meet the increasing public demand that the schools accept accountability for their heavy responsibilities.

This is a book that furnishes fuel for debate among administrators and teachers because Lessinger shows the inadequacy, often the fallacy, of many of our cherished assumptions. It will also be widely read because it clarifies much of the vague and ambiguous discussions regarding "performance contracts," "professional incentives," and "accountability."

Ralph W. Tyler
Director Emeritus
Center for Advanced Study
July 27, 1970   in the Behavioral Sciences

A
Bill of Rights
for Students,
Taxpayers,
and
Educators

Chapter 1

*I*F ONE AIRPLANE in every four crashed between takeoff and landing, people would refuse to fly. If one automobile in every four went out of control and caused a fatal accident or permanent injury, Detroit would be closed down tomorrow.

Our schools — which produce a more important product than airplanes or automobiles — somehow fail one youngster in four. And so far we have not succeeded in preventing the social and economic fatalities every school dropout represents.

For each child thus failed by his school, all of us pay a price in taxes and in social unrest, and the child himself is deprived of his chance to develop his potential.

However, thanks to a set of recent developments, so far little noted, we can now sharply cut this waste of lives and money. In fact, American educators now have an opportunity so far-reaching that, with a push from the public, *we can transform our schools within this decade.*

This opportunity springs from several sources: from a new and sophisticated process of management that defines educational goals in *measurable* terms; from stimulating innovations discovered by new alliances among local schools, the federal government, and private enterprise; from testing programs that can be used at low political, social, and economic risk to discover what actually works; from the ability to avoid bureaucratic delay and put effective programs in the classrooms immediately; and from the growing acceptance of the idea that the schools, like other sectors of our society, are accountable to the public for what they do — or fail to do.

These developments make possible a new process to bring to the improvement of education the same ingenuity, craft, and realism that got us to the moon. In this sense, the process is an example of engineering or, more broadly, a method of management that uses engineering insights on which leading firms rely — but which our schools have largely ignored.

What is Happening In Our Schools Now?

Many of our children urgently need the benefits of educational engineering. Performance statistics in the inner-city schools reveal that many children read three years or more below the national norm, that in some schools up to seventy percent of the students drop out before graduation, that few graduates can compose an essay in acceptable English or perform basic arithmetic operations. Studies show that many children in the ghetto have no more than a vague, distorted notion about life outside their own impoverished world. In short, they are prepared for nothing but another generation of failure.[1] For the well-being of our society, we cannot afford to perpetuate this parody of education. Many parents, disturbed by years of vague talk from the schools, are demanding performance, not more promises.

So far the answer has been to appropriate more money. The very schools that most need additional funds, however, are often the least equipped to use it. Unable to break out of a pattern of failing programs, these schools often merely supply a slightly less degraded version of what they have already been doing. No wonder that Congress and the president are now asking what good was done by the billions of federal dollars spent on elementary and secondary education in the past five years.

Three Basic Rights of Democratic Education

The reform of our schools will take additional money—large amounts of it—but money alone is not enough. In order to assure educational results, we ought to start by recognizing three basic rights in modern education.

First, each child has a right to be taught what he needs to know in order to take a productive, rewarding part in our society. Second, the taxpayer and his elected representative have a right to know what educational results are produced by a given expenditure. And third, the schools have a right to be able to draw on talent, enterprise, and technology from all sectors of society instead of being restricted to educators' overburdened resources.

1. In spite of the need, the high school at present is failing to serve effectively more than half the youth who are of high school age," wrote Ralph W. Tyler in "Investing in Better Schools," *Agenda for the Nation* (Washington, D.C.: The Brookings Institution, 1968, page 213.) "For most of our citizens, the American educational system is among the most successful in the history of the world," wrote President Nixon on March 3, 1970. "But for a portion of our population, it has never delivered on its promises." (Special message on educational reform.)

In the absence of these rights, consider the dreary alternatives. Without the first of these educational rights, our society will continue to turn out millions of young people who feel useless, cheated, and resentful. The consequences, as we have begun to see, are ominous; and the human waste is inexcusable. Without the second of these rights, the public and its officials are deprived of hard facts about the quality of educational results produced by the tax money we supply. Without these facts, how can we judge which programs to support? And until the third right — the right of schools to form new alliances with the sources of innovation — is recognized in practice, we will continue to suffer the result of a closed educational bureaucracy.

The Child's Right to Learn

Let us consider each of these basic rights in turn, starting with the right of each child to know the basic skills without which he would fail in modern society.[2] This right to know is not satisfied by providing a school desk for the child, putting books in front of him, and having a teacher go through the steps of a specified curriculum. It is satisfied only by objective proof that, after going to school, he can exercise the necessary skills and apply his knowledge. We are talking about demonstrable results, not merely ten or twelve years' exposure to a program that may offer a measure of success to some of the children (or even to most of them). In a sophisticated technological society, each child has a right to be taught a mastery of the essentials, by whatever means are necessary.

Stated in this way, the point seems indisputable. Who would argue that, as a matter of policy, we ought to allow a significant fraction of our children to go into the adult world without the means for earning a decent living or being responsible citizens? Yet that is what we do. In other spheres we do much better. In building rockets we engage in "zero-defect" programs of quality assurance, for we know that if a single part fails, the rocket fails. Can we not find ways to do as well for our children? Similarly, medical research has made immense advances not by putting all

2. These basic skills obviously include the ability to read. In September 1969, in a speech to the School Boards Association in San Francisco, the former U.S. Commissioner of Education, James E. Allen, Jr., proclaimed "the right to read" as a chief goal for the next decade; and in March 1970, President Nixon endorsed this goal, observing in his special message on educational reform that "the basic ability to read is a right that should be denied to no one, and the pleasures found in books and libraries should be available to all."

of its emphasis on ordinary or common illnesses, but by refusing to ignore any illness, no matter how unusual or difficult to treat. The point, of course, is not that a child is a rocket component or his ignorance a disease, but that educators ought to show no less ingenuity or persistence than engineers and doctors, no less devotion to the most difficult cases.

In 1965 Congress passed the far-reaching Elementary and Secondary Education Act. Its purpose was to widen the opportunity for quality education, and its ultimate goal to assure basic competence for every student. Sponsors of the act questioned the assumption that in any educational system some children will inevitably fail. They asked, for example, what is the point of grading a student with A, B, C, D, or F on his reading if we know that he stands no chance of making it today unless he can read? If he is given a D or F, the child is said to have failed, but from the standpoint of society, the school has failed; and society as well as the student will have to pay dearly for that failure.

While grades may serve as a diagnostic mark to show who needs special help, they can easily lead to a set of false assumptions based on the bell-shaped distribution curve that is often used to allocate grades from A to F to a "normal" group of students. The symmetry of this curve leads us to believe that this system is fair and orderly, until we stop to realize that the children on the wrong side of the slope—the ones slipping down toward F—lack the ability to operate in modern society. How can we tolerate a system in which roughly a quarter of the children (and in some schools a much larger fraction) are *expected* to fail or barely to make the grade? Is this the best our schools can do?

The Education Act of 1965 assumes that we can do better. Billions of dollars have already been appropriated on the grounds that, for the sake of our future, we must do better. Under the new mandate, schools are asked to give each student the competence he needs, regardless of the difficulties; and that means regardless of his initial or apparent interest, his cultural background, his home life, or his ability as measured by culture-bound tests. In effect, this act asks the schools *to guarantee the acquisition of necessary skills.* This guarantee has never been more important and perhaps never, for ghetto schools, more difficult to give. Sharp-eyed observers of these schools have pointed out the difficulties and the failures. Now we must decide whether to honor the guarantee or let it lapse.

Compared with others, our public education system has done wonders, carrying a large proportion of our children to a high (though vaguely measured) level of achievement. Now, however, the demands placed on certain crucial parts of this system have clearly outrun its capabilities. The result, especially in many of the inner-city schools, amounts to nothing less than a scandal.

When a scandal arises, we usually seek someone to blame, or when threatened in our community pride or pocketbook, we may try to pretend that nothing is wrong, or that no remedy is possible. We have reacted in each of these ways to the cases of failing schools in the ghetto and elsewhere. Some of us have blamed the children, saying they must be stupid, or we have called their parents irresponsible. Others have condemned the educators who administer those schools, although they face skimpy budgets, low morale, apparently bored students, and community resentment. Many of us who live in the suburbs or in thriving smaller cities manage to ignore the problems of ghetto schools, at least most of the time; and when we do listen to educators, they usually offer not a reliable plan for reform, but merely a plea for higher taxes. On the other hand, school officials may regard it a false economy when voters defeat a school-bond or tax-raising issue, as they have been doing frequently, or when the president vetoes an education bill, but they might also profitably ask why public confidence in their leadership seems to have declined.

To some extent these educators are unfairly blamed for problems caused by large social movements that Americans, on the whole, seem to favor: movements such as increasing urbanization, the rapid development of technology, and even the effort to bring excluded minorities, especially black people, into the mainstream of our society. Whatever their value, such movements also cause problems, or, as in the case of ghetto schools, call long-standing problems to our attention.

We Americans have always looked to schools as the key to social mobility, but now an education is necessary to survive at all, except as a perpetual ward of the state or a minimal contributor to the economy. In this unhappy situation educators can plead that their job was never more perplexing, that much of the public refuses to recognize the difficulty of educating children whose life teaches them to expect failure, and that as a consequence the schools most in need of help often get the least. All of these things are true. In order to win a sympathetic hearing, however, these

educators are going to have to show results. After all, we judge a
school not by whether it runs its own bureaucracy according to the
rules, by whether the staff have all taken certain college courses,
or by whether it provides each class with a textbook and a teacher.
Essentially we judge a school, or ought to judge it, by whether its
students gain certain skills and knowledge that can be measured
against some set of standards or judgments, and by the cost of
producing these gains.

In short, then, we pose two questions: Can the school guarantee
the acquisition of basic skills? And does it use the most economical means to this end?

The Taxpayer's Right to Know

Let us now consider the second of the educational rights stated
above, the right of each taxpayer and his elected representative to
know what educational results are produced by a given expenditure. In the past four years the federal government has spent $4.3
billion on Title I of the Elementary and Secondary Education Act
of 1965, which is a program for poverty-stricken children who are
doing badly in school. According to a *New York Times* survey of
this program, very few school districts have objective test data that
shows substantial improvement in the skills of these children.
In some places, tests showed no interruption at all of the typical
pattern of failure in which poor children from both city slums and
rural areas fall further and further behind national achievement
norms and ultimately drop out of school. And in a majority of
states and localities surveyed, officials said they simply did not
have any conclusive test results by which to gauge the effects of
most Title I programs.[3]

We literally do not know what educational results have been
produced by that $4.3 billion. Should we continue to spend sums of
this magnitude in any area of government without knowing what
benefits, if any, we are buying?

With the advent of major federal aid to education, taxpayers
increasingly ask, "What are we getting for our money?" Traditional answers in terms of resources employed, teachers available, and buildings provided are no longer sufficient. The public
wants to know, for a start, whether young people can read, can get
and hold a job, can go as far in higher education as their abilities

---

3. *New York Times*, December 28, 1969, story by William K. Stevens.

warrant. This is a call for accountability for results, a growing demand for changes in the way that schools are managed.[4]

The Schools' Right to Teach

If schools are to be held accountable for results, they must develop a new approach to their basic mission. In the first place, they must define their output no longer as teaching done, but as learning proven. In a haphazard or partial way, some schools do offer proof of results, as when they report the average score of their college applicants who take the so-called national achievement tests. For purposes of accountability, however, this kind of data is severely deficient. It applies only to students with hope of further education, not to those who drop out or who barely make it through high school. And it measures the results of twelve years of schooling, not of any particular class or program. In contrast, what we need is data for all children that shows the educational gain produced by specific sequences of teaching.

Linking Learning to its Costs

Once the output of schools is measured in proven learning instead of resources allocated or teaching done, the next step is to relate learning to its cost. In theory we can easily compare the money spent and the result achieved. We simply keep accounts of the cost of a specific teaching sequence and measure the change in performance against a standardized evaluation given before and after it. This is seldom accurately done except in formal experiments. Now we must extend this kind of calculation to cover wide areas of teaching, especially the acquisition of basic skills such as reading.

4. In leaving the San Mateo Union High School District to become Associate U.S. Commissioner for Elementary and Secondary Education, the author told a press conference that he hoped to have school districts bidding for federal dollars on the basis of which suppliers could offer more guaranteed results, as with other government contracts. "We might even offer a bonus clause and give more money if they produce better results than they anticipated," the author said in September 1968. "At least it holds them accountable to get results where many federal programs today do not." (See stories by Ron Moskowitz in the *San Francisco Chronicle*, September 19, 1968, and in *Education News*, October 7, 1968. In his special message on educational reform, President Nixon stated on March 3, 1970, that "school administrators and school teachers alike are responsible for their performance, and it is in their interest as well as the interests of their pupils that they be held accountable." Educational accomplishment, said the president, should be measured "by the results achieved in relation to the actual situation of the particular school and the particular set of pupils." (*New York Times*, March 4, 1970, page 28).

True, education also has objectives that are difficult to measure or even to define clearly, such as "maturity" or "high motivation." But the fact that education is greater than the sum of its measurable parts should not deter us from obtaining reliable data on those parts that *do* lend themselves to definition and measurement. In concentrating on these parts, such as the basic skills, we must of course make sure that our instruments and judgments accurately assess the range of things that are important to know, not only what is easiest to measure.

Once we have standardized, reliable data on the cost of producing a variety of educational results, using a variety of methods, our legislators and school officials will at last be able to draw up budgets based on facts instead of on vague assertions. Through the knowledge gained in this process of management, we will also be able to hold the schools accountable for results. For example, in awarding most kinds of federal grants to schools, we now specify objectives very loosely and depend mainly on the agency spending the money for the assessment of its results. Needless to say, this system of grant-giving leads to subjective progress reports in which the optimism is largely unverified. How can an agency be held accountable when the purpose of the grant is loosely stated and the results are self-assessed, often without proper testing?

In financial matters, we require a business or a public agency to open its books to an independent auditor, instead of assuring us of its own honesty and fiscal competence. Why should we require any less with regard to educational results? In business we judge the effectiveness of a firm by its profit, by investment return, and by other financial indicators. In a non-profit agency such as a school, we judge its effectiveness according to the benefits experienced by its clients (or in the case of education, its students). Although these benefits are more difficult to measure than profit in a business, we can assess them far more accurately, usefully, and consistently than we now do.

Provision for detailed public auditing of educational results will bolster educators' professional credentials. Ultimately there is only one test of professional competence: proof of results. For example, if an attorney loses as many cases as he wins, he will soon have none but the most ignorant or impecunious clients. Neither specialized education nor experience by itself validates his claim to special wisdom. Professionalism, in other words, goes hand-in-hand with accountability, with clear-cut proof of performance. In general, educators so far have rested their claim less on assured results than on their university credits, years of service, and probity in administering public funds.

Our public elementary and secondary schools enroll 44 million students, employ 1.9 million teachers, and spend over $30 billion in tax funds annually. We have all kinds of measurements of where that money goes: we can pin down per-capita expenditures in any school district in the country, state how much any of them spend for construction and interest payments on borrowed money, and enumerate pupil-teacher ratios until the sun goes down. But all of these figures, useful as they are for some purposes, refer exclusively to financial inputs rather than educational outputs. We have virtually no measurement of the results that our vast enterprise yields. For example, we do not know what the average cost of increasing a youngster's reading ability by one year is: all we know is what it costs to keep him seated for one year with a textbook and a teacher. Many of the available indexes measure our competence as financial managers; but how many of them evaluate our effectiveness as educational managers? It would make much more sense if we moved from the concept of per-pupil cost to the concept of *learning-unit cost,* and focused on the cost of skill acquisition rather than on the cost of maintaining children in schools.

Where Have We Failed?

We have made few such moves to measure our results, however. And our dereliction as educators is all the more embarrassing because ample proof of our failures is evident. Today about one of every four American children drops out of school somewhere between fifth grade and high school graduation. In 1965, one of every four eighteen-year-old males failed the mental test for induction into the service. And a growing number of parents, reacting to information such as this, have decided that instead of labeling a large fraction of children as hopelessly stupid, we ought to ask whether the educators in charge of these children are competent to perform their task, and whether the methods they use are adequate.

Why did these assessments of our failures as educators have to come from outside the school system, rather than from within? Why have we not been sufficiently alert to the symptoms of failure so that we could learn to cure it? An alarming number of American children are not being taught the basic facts and skills they need to function in our society. Is it any wonder that critics such as Paul Goodman and Edgar Friedenberg feel that many students who are being failed by the present system would be better off on the street than in the classroom? Or that some parents feel that rank amateurs could do no worse a job of running a school than the self-styled pros, at least in the ghetto? In refusing to give our clients proof of performance while they gathered their own proof of our flops, we as educators set the stage for the raucous and bitter confrontation of power blocs that marks inner-city education today.

Moreover, we have eroded our own claim to professionalism. We have dissipated that confidence the public once reposed in its educators. And we have nearly erased those distinctions between the specialist's knowledge and the layman's concern that are required for the success both of democratic control and of professional operation. The most important aspect of this melancholy process is not that educators feel threatened—for we *ought* to feel threatened—but rather that many aspects of the educational endeavor do require a professional's knowledge. How can educators extend their effective knowledge and thus recover their authority? Upon the answer hinges not only their prestige, of course, but also the success of our children and, ultimately, our society.

What Can We Do?

So far we have outlined a goal and a working principle: next we will propose a method. Stated most simply, our goal is the *guaranteed* acquisition of basic skills by *all* of our children. In this sense every kid can be a winner!

We can reach this goal through the concept of accountability for educational results, based on the independent educational audit. A goal without a method for achieving it, however, leads to nothing but frustrated expectations, as we know from recent unhappy experience; and holding the schools accountable will lead to nothing but despair on the part of educators unless we also provide a flexible, effective, and usable process for securing the necessary innovations. We have discovered that, in reforming a demoralized school, more money in itself is seldom sufficient. What the schools also need is a process of *educational engineering*.

Engineering for Education

Everybody knows that in engineering we define exactly what we want, then bring together resources and technology in such a way as to assure those results. In applying this process to the design of education, we are proposing, of course, not that schools treat students as if they were unfinished products in a factory, but rather that we devote to the fashioning of educational programs at least as much imagination, skill, and discipline as we routinely apply to the building of a color TV set. If the educational program is badly engineered, as it is so often now, the children will receive little from it.

When a program in the schools is well engineered, it will meet several tests: it will require educational planners to specify, in measurable terms, what they are trying to accomplish. It will provide for an independent audit of results. It will allow taxpayers and their representatives to judge the educational payoff of a given appropriation. It will stimulate a continuing process of innovation, not merely a one-shot reform. It will call forth educational ideas, talent, and technology from all sectors of our society, not only from within a particular school system. It will allow schools to experiment with new programs at limited risk and adopt the best of them promptly. Above all, it will guarantee results in terms of what students can actually do. In this sense, educational engineering is not a single program, but a technique for the management of change. With the demands and pressures on our schools, they will undoubtedly change: the question is whether we will run that change or be run by it.

Managing for Change
Let us consider the third of the educational rights stated above, the right of schools to enter new alliances that can assure the funds and skill necessary for the development, testing, and introduction of effective programs.

The organization of most school systems cuts them off from sophisticated, flexible innovation. In the inner city, for example, many schools, like the families they exist to serve, struggle along on starvation budgets. The energy of the staff is absorbed largely in keeping discipline, overcoming a sense of boredom and hopelessness, and going through the motions of teaching. How can such a school possibly change? All its energy goes into barely surviving. In many schools that enjoy a somewhat higher level of support and morale, the educational program is more effective, insofar as we can judge from crude indicators, but it is no less resistant to improvement. Even when we appropriate more funds, the structure of the educational program seldom changes, no matter how urgently change is needed. What is the cause of this inertia?

Part of the answer lies in the way we manage our schools, including the way we grant federal funds. Consider the economic centrality of our elementary and secondary schools. Together they form an enterprise that does close to 40 billion dollars' worth of business annually, which serves as a supplier for every aspect of our economy as well as for higher education. Its clients include every person who pays taxes.

In our technological age, what would we ordinarily think of an enterprise that spends only a fraction of one percent of its income on research and development? That often fails effectively to apply the knowledge which it does have? That is so labor-intensive that it spends, on the average, less than four percent of its budget for materials, equipment, and supplies? What future do we predict for an enterprise run by people who lack training in sophisticated management techniques, who exercise little creative control over their personnel, and who seldom know exactly what effect they are having? Unfortunately, our public schools make up such an enterprise. Apart from a relatively small fraction of children whose parents pay double to send them to a private or parochial school, this enterprise has a monopoly on elementary and secondary education. Without the tax revenue it receives, how long would this monopoly survive?

In order to justify its dominant claim on our public education dollar, this enterprise must begin to account for its spending not only in terms of fiscal honesty, as it has long done, but also in terms of proven educational results. In order to produce these results, school managers must renew their institutions by forming new alliances with those outside the schools who can develop, package, test, introduce, manage, and verify new methods for the guaranteed acquisition of necessary skills. To facilitate development of these alliances, we must learn to think of education as a complex, adaptable kind of business, not as the self-contained institutions of less demanding times, much less as the little red schoolhouse of the past.

Yet many in our schools still regard them as if education were a kind of cottage industry rather than, in effect, a modern corporation. How else can we account for some of the lingering beliefs and practices in our schools, beliefs deeply rooted in the past and relatively unchanged in the face of massive assault? For example, a great many people believe that when business practices enter the school system, the quality of education goes out the window. Others suspect that systems thinking is a scheme for teacher-proofing education, replacing people with computers, reducing everything to numbers, and valuing costs over people. It is also commonly believed that efficiency is a cult that destroys the funda-mental purpose of schools, that performance criteria inevitably restrict individual freedom, and that it is good to gather data but not necessarily important to use it.

Together these beliefs suggest that among educational person-nel the word *management* has far less value than it does in other fields. Why do some of us prefer the word "administration"? Does it suggest a more settled, less troublesome existence? Nobody wants trouble, but when it comes, as it has to many schools, we must have the techniques for replacing unsuccessful programs with new programs that work. A failing school, no matter how bravely "administered," is still a failing school. To get the results that parents, their representatives, and even students are rightly demanding, we must learn how to change.

The need confronts us but the structure of education is slow to respond. As John Gardner notes, ". . . we are poor at problem-solving that requires the revision of social structures, the renewal of institutions, the invention of new human arrangements.

"Not only are problems in this realm exceedingly complex, but in some cases we are rather strongly motivated *not* to solve them. Solving them would endanger old, familiar ways of doing things."[5]

Painful stalemates in public policy are caused by the tendency of outworn institutions both to resist reforms from within and, in the case of a near monopoly, to discourage the rise of competitors. For example, some people who could help transform our schools take up other careers because they see no hope; and among those already in education, many find their ideas ground down by bureaucratic delay, by lack of funds for development, by admin-istrators who say they have no room for maneuver. How can ideas flourish in such a setting? Seldom does the local education author-ity preserve a free space where programs can be created, tried, and improved for general use.

Obviously, then, one method for renewing the schools would

---

5. John Gardner, *No Easy Victories* (New York: Harper and Row, 1968), page 27.

rely on the liberation of energies, skills, and ideas within the local district. Much can be done in this way, but it requires leadership, hard cash, and staff time. If a local education authority would reserve as little as one percent of its budget as developmental capital, and would offer to support experimental programs developed by its own personnel, the schools might at least escape the familiar cycle of drawn-out studies, official inaction, and the renaming of (or tinkering with) clearly decrepit programs. Action might then replace the words which serve, too often, as our only solace.

Educators need money set aside for the purpose of stimulating competition and improvement in the system. Money available for responsible investment in teachers, students, and non-school-affiliated persons and organizations to produce results in the form of student accomplishment is the energy of accountability. Development capital is desperately needed in education—otherwise good ideas never get beyond the stage of talk. Business typically budgets amounts ranging from three to fifteen percent for research and development in order to produce better products, better service, more sales, or more capability to produce these items. Educators need the same resources to act as entrepreneurs for student accomplishment. With a sum of money regularly available annually, they can apply the forces that have been so productive in the private sector to problems in the public sector.

Another method for improving education is to undermine the dominance of the public schools. Under one plan now being studied by a group in Cambridge, Massachusetts, each parent would be given a voucher representing his child's share of the public-school budget—a voucher that could then be "spent" at any public school chosen by the parent, or at a private school, or even, in one version of the plan, at a profit-making school established in response to the voucher market.[6] The local education authority would reimburse each school for the vouchers it collected, with the public schools competing on the same basis as any other supplier of education.

Like the plan for educational engineering outlined in this book, the voucher scheme would stimulate a healthy competition, leading to innovations we urgently need; but unlike our plan, the voucher scheme could easily weaken inner-city public schools and induce a proliferation of schools representing narrow interests of

6. *The National Observer*, December 2, 1970, story by John Morton.

many kinds and isolating groups of children who now learn to know one another in the public schools.[7] Whatever virtues are promised by some version of the voucher scheme, we must keep in mind that designing a system radically different from our basic traditional school system may result in further fragmentation of our society.

How can we both preserve the unity of our schools and give them full access to the same diversity of talent and methods sought by proponents of the voucher scheme? Essentially the answer is simple, but our tradition of the school as a self-contained institution has kept us from recognizing the opportunity to draw on outside help, especially help in fostering innovation. Few American business firms decline to take advantage of advice, special services, discoveries, or pilot programs supplied by professionals or by other firms. When a company needs assistance or sees an opportunity, it calls on lawyers, management consultants, technical specialists, inventors, or on other enterprises that have a product or process to offer. How can our schools gain a similar freedom to reach outside the confines of their own structures?

Contracting for Performance

We can learn to regard the school not as a self-sufficient, closed system, dependent only on textbook publishers and desk suppliers, but as an open system in which many services are orchestrated by professional managers responsible, as always, to elected local boards. Where are these services to be found? If development capital is made available within a local education authority, the staff itself can develop some of the new services. Others can be drawn from the many companies and non-profit institutions that are now starting to offer instructional services, based on advanced materials, technology, and motivational programs.

With appropriate patterns of federal and state funding, and with modern management support provided to a local education authority, these instructional systems can be brought into a school promptly and, when their success is assured, taken over by the

7. The idea of vouchers for schooling was first put forth by the economist Milton Friedman in Robert A. Solo (ed.), *Economics and the Public Interest* (New Brunswick, N.J.: Rutgers University Press, 1955). Among recent articles in favor of the idea, see especially "Is the Public School Obsolete?" by Christopher Jencks, *The Public Interest*, Winter 1966, pages 18-27; and among those that oppose a voucher scheme, see "In Defense of the 'Harmful Monopoly,'" by Edward J. Fox and William B. Levenson, *Phi Delta Kappan*, November 1969, pages 131-35.

local staff for continuing operation. If a given program fails to measure up, the school can quickly drop it with no disruption of the
normal program or of the pattern of staffing. When a school contracts for innovation, the risks of failure (and, should a failure
occur, its effects) are sharply limited. This insurance against educational shortcomings is provided through what industry calls a
performance contract, a powerful and flexible instrument of which
educators are now starting to realize the potential.

Essentially, a performance contract is an agreement by a firm
or individual to produce specified results by a certain date, using
acceptable methods, for a set fee. The parties may agree in advance that, if the conditions are not met by that date, the firm must
continue its efforts, for no additional fee, until they are met; and
also that if the requirements are exceeded, either by early completion or by a higher level of achievement, the fee will be increased
by specified amounts. Thus, in a contract for educational services,
the school has a guarantee that for the budgeted expenditure, students will acquire certain skills, as measured by an independent
auditor; and the supplier of the services has a strong incentive not
only to meet but to exceed the contractual requirements.

Known for decades in American business, this concept now appeals to hard-pressed educators in part because it recognizes each
of the three rights discussed in this chapter. It allows the school to
supplement the efforts of its own staff by obtaining help, especially
for new programs, from an exciting variety of sources. It provides
parents and their elected officials with reliable, detailed figures on
the level and costs of educational results.[8]

But what exactly does performance contracting involve? In
order to use it effectively, a local education authority forms temporary alliances with several outside agencies. First, it needs a
source of funds earmarked for educational development. School
districts that are both prosperous and farsighted can raise some
of this money from their own local budgets, but most districts will
depend heavily on grants from state and federal agencies.

Second, performance contracting requires a management support group that can help local officials specify exactly what educa-

8. The promise of performance contracting sounds almost too great to be true, but with help
from the U.S. Office of Education, it is now being tried in the schools of Texarkana, a community that, as the name suggests, lies on the border of Arkansas and Texas. Described below
in more detail, this pilot program has already led to widespread interest within educational
circles and to applications for grants from many other cities, large and small, that want to improve their schools promptly and efficiently through performance contracting.

tional results are sought; in writing a request for bids from firms willing to do the job; in negotiating with and evaluating these firms; in drawing up the contract; and in dealing with the chosen firm.

Third, the local authority needs the services of an independent educational auditor who will assess the children before and after the program and make a public report. This report will determine whether the contractor has met all of the requirements and, if so, whether he is entitled to the incentive payments for exceeding the minimum standards.

Last, but hardly least, the plan requires that various firms or other groups bid vigorously for the contract, tailoring their resources to the stated needs of the local school. Early experience indicates that a wide variety of firms in the information and knowledge industry will assign top-level talent to the preparation of detailed, ingenious proposals for the consideration of local school boards. And growing skepticism in Washington about conventional programs for improving the schools may be a sign that more federal funds may be earmarked for performance contracts in education (and perhaps elsewhere).

Troubled by money shortages, racial tension, and dubious aspects of the new youth culture, educators nonetheless have reason for hope. According to Donald Rumsfeld, director of the Office of Economic Opportunity and Cabinet member, such a process could indeed revolutionize education in this country. He said, "Historically we have measured our concern by asking how many millions we spend, how many textbooks we buy, how many schools we build. But these are all inputs. They don't tell us anything about the impact on human lives."[9]

If educators can master the process outlined above — a process for engineering programs that work — overburdened educators will regain a spirit of excitement and mastery that has flagged in recent years. Where the viability of public schools is now in question, as in the ghetto, the process of educational engineering can revitalize a central American institution. It can save society the long-term cost of allowing its schools to define millions of children as "failures." It can assure that as taxpayers we get our dollar's worth. And it can stimulate private industry, which so far has given our schools little more than books and bricks, to expand its contribution to the education of our children.

9. New York *Times*, May 15, 1970, story by Jack Rosenthal.

Educational
Engineering

Chapter 2

a GOOD ENGINEER begins by challenging assumptions. He refuses to believe that something is impossible merely because it has never been done or because people say there is no way to do it or because it would upset established ways. The good engineer, in the field of education as elsewhere, starts with a goal to be achieved, not with the dead weight of precedent or unexamined beliefs. Like the runner who finally broke the four-minute mile, he knows that the limits of possibility are stretched not solely by pushing from within, but by setting an outside goal and doing what is necessary to reach it. In track competition, once the four-minute mark was set, other runners soon matched the feat, mainly because they had learned that it was possible. Their assumptions had changed.

Changing Our Assumptions About Education

In education most of us share deep-seated assumptions about something called aptitude or the ability to learn. What is aptitude? Nearly all of our educators treat it, in effect, as a rough prediction of grades that, in turn, are supposed to show how much a child has learned. (Any discrepancy between this prediction and the eventual grade is explained as "under-achievement" or, less often, as "over-achievement.") After a given course, tests generally show that some children have learned significantly more than the others, and that a certain group, sometimes quite large, has barely scraped through. According to these test results, we assign grades, with most falling somewhere in the middle of the scale and, except in rare cases, with relatively few at either extreme. On the basis of these grades some children learn to regard themselves as good students, others as fair, and the remainder as poor or impossible.

We all know about this system because we went through it, and if we did well enough to be reading this book or working now in a school, few of us give the system a second thought, except to increase "fairness" or "accuracy" in assigning grades. After all, nobody denies that some children are "brighter" than others or that some work harder, so we continue to sort children into the "B" slot or the "F" slot with the impartiality of a postal clerk who separates the dead letters from the first-class mail. Of course, we try to improve the program of the school so that everyone learns more, whatever his level of "aptitude": for the good students we may offer advanced placement courses, and for others some manner of "enrichment" or "compensatory education." Whatever the quality of education, however, we continue to sort the students into various bins according to what they have been able to learn, as measured by our tests; and in most cases the children adopt these grades and scores into their self-definitions.

Changing the Approach to Aptitude

This whole approach to aptitude, so familiar that it seems part of the natural order, is now being challenged. The critics agree that students differ in their aptitude, but they argue persuasively that we ought to define aptitude *not* as the degree of mastery a student will attain within a given course, but rather as a function of the amount of time he needs to attain full mastery of learning a task.[1] This new definition of aptitude turns our attention away from the weary routine of sorting out children according to how many questions they can answer after a fixed course. It sets as a goal for the end of an educational cycle not merely fair grading of the class, but each student's mastery of skills. In other words, as applied to the acquisition of basic skills, the new definition of aptitude points out that, apart from a very small percentage of children, every student can earn a grade of "A."

Obviously some students can master a skill such as reading more quickly than others, and some will be quite slow, but if the curriculum is adapted to these differences, every child can learn to read or to calculate or to master any of the other skills essential to a productive life in our society. And when he does master it he deserves an "A" — or rather, since letter grades are contaminated with the old assumptions, he deserves a certificate describing the skills he has mastered, a reflection of the competence warranty. What matters most with regard to a particular skill is not how long

---

1. John Carroll, "A Model of School Learning," *Teachers' College Record* 64 (1963): 723-33; and Benjamin S. Bloom, "Learning for Mastery," *Evaluation Comment* 1 (May 1968): 1-12.

a child took to master it or the type of training he received, but the fact that he now possesses the skill.

What happens when we accept the new definition of aptitude? Instead of a fixed program in which each child learns what he can, we set a goal of basic mastery for everyone and offer whatever programs are necessary to meet that goal. Instead of grades we give diagnostic tests to help us decide which program each child needs; and at the end of the process we might award skill warranties instead of the increasingly dubious "diploma." With regard to the basic skills, instead of labeling some children as losers, we assume that with appropriate training every kid will finish as a winner. In this sense, the schools should treat learning to read not as a race straight to the top of a mountain but as the ability to get there, one way or another, at a variety of paces.

As long as schools cling to the old distorted notion of aptitude, they will be satisfied to grade children on whether they can mount from one level of reading to the next in the average time allowed within the standard pattern of instruction. If a child does badly, he is said to have "low aptitude" or maybe he "lacks motivation" and he ends up with a chronic case of "dyslexia" (which is a fancy way of saying that the school has not taught him how to read), or he goes through the rest of his life with a "reading problem." The failure, however, is seldom blamed on the school. Somehow it is usually blamed on a condition such as social background for which the school has no responsibility.

This is often done with the best of intentions as a step toward providing special programs for children who are presumed to have special needs. Thus, in referring to some children, we speak of the "culturally deprived" or the "socially disadvantaged." In practice, however, these labels function less as descriptive terms than as value judgments which often surface, submerge, and reappear in new guises. Such labels are not useful in dealing with the problem. On the contrary, they tend to mask the ineffectiveness of educational programs and provide us with a rationalization when we find that our methods do not work. If the methods work for some children, we say, what is the matter with the others?

The futility of such labeling was amusingly depicted by the satirist Jules Fieffer. In his series of drawings an impoverished, elderly gentleman reflects as follows: "I used to think I was *poor.* . . . Then they told me I wasn't poor, I was *needy.* . . . Then they told me it was self-defeating to think of myself as needy,

I was *deprived.* . . . Then they told me deprived was a bad image, I was *underprivileged.* . . . Then they told me underprivileged was overused, I was *disadvantaged.* . . . I still don't have a dime, but I have a great vocabulary!"

Changing Educator's Expectations

Lest we airily dismiss such labeling as a harmless exercise in substituting one term for another, consider that categorizing certain children and their parents as "deprived," "disadvantaged," "uninterested," or "lazy" actually leads, in most cases, to corresponding behaviors on the part of both the labeler and the group being labeled. No matter how well-meaning we are in using some of these phrases, they are often taken to imply a chronic condition, a sort of social fate that may well be passed along to the next generation and the one after that. Sympathetic terms such as "disadvantaged," no less than dubious judgments such as "lazy," can function as a self-fulfilling prophecy. Often in subtle ways, we act *as if* these children will have trouble or will probably fail, and the children become discouraged as they acquire, often subconsciously, the fear and then the expectation of defeat.

The tragic consequences of this phenomenon were dramatically brought to our attention by the experiments on teacher expectations conducted in South San Francisco by Dr. Robert Rosenthal and described in his book, *Pygmalion in the Classroom.* In that experiment teachers were led to believe at the beginning of a school year that certain of their pupils could be expected to show considerable academic improvement during that year. The teachers thought these predictions were based on tests that had been administered to the student body at the end of the preceding school year. In fact, the children designated as potential "spurters" had been chosen at random with no reference to test results or to grades. Nonetheless, intelligence tests given after the experiment had been in progress for several months indicated that, on the whole, the randomly chosen children had improved more than the rest.[2]

Rosenthal's study has been well publicized and widely discussed, but have we taken full account of its findings? Keep in mind that the experimental group was chosen randomly and thus, contrary

---

2. Robert Rosenthal, *Pygmalion in the Classroom* (New York: Holt, Rhinehart and Winston, Inc., 1968).

to the teachers' belief, was no different from the control group. When teachers were asked to describe students in each group, however, they found members of the experimental group more attractive, better adjusted, more appealing, and less in need of social approval than members of the control group. Naturally, some of this group also gained in IQ during the year, and Dr. Rosenthal discovered that, on the average, the more a student in the control group gained, the *less* favorably he was described by his teacher. This inverse ratio between high rate of unexpected pupil gain and an unfavorable teacher attitude provides us with a devastating portrait of the persistence of low expectations on the part of teachers, regardless of student performance. In other words, the teachers knew that members of the control group were not supposed to do well, and they apparently regarded students who forced an exception to that rule as somehow uppity.

If we consider this finding about teacher expectations together with the charges that IQ tests are culture-bound and often fail to detect the full potential of some children, we are faced with the possibility that certain schools, in the words of their critics, actually make children stupid. A sharp-eyed school teacher, John Holt, has even leveled the much broader charge that children actually decline in enthusiasm, curiosity, and confidence from the very day they start formal school. He sees the present school system as a negative force in learning.[3] This is a striking and terrible indictment. What we are saying is much less broad: we are seriously raising the question whether certain schools inadvertently lead many of their students to define themselves as stupid, at least with regard to academic work. We are referring mainly to the schools in depressed areas that are often charged with serving as little more than custodial institutions.

To the extent that this charge is true, the situation is intolerable, but is it so surprising? After all, if teachers are put in a frustrating or even frightening situation, they are no less inclined than the rest of us to welcome a scapegoat. Whether the scapegoat is the supposedly stupid or recalcitrant child or the environment of which he is said to be a victim, the result is the same: the school is excused for the failure. If the child is "disadvantaged," what can his poor school do?

The answer, according to the noted educator and sociologist

---

3. John Holt, *How Children Fail* (New York: Pitman Publishing Co., 1964).

Kenneth B. Clark, is that with the proper expectations and programs, our schools can teach every child what he needs to know.[4]

In the past few years our eyes have been opened to this humiliation not only by senior educators such as Clark but also by a new breed of writers, teachers, and former teachers who, as they say, "tell it like it is." Such books as Nat Hentoff's *Our Children are Dying*, John Holt's *How Children Fail*, Herbert Kohl's *36 Children*, and the award-winning *Death at an Early Age* by Jonathan Kozol, present devastating indictments of current classroom practices. Grindingly dull, irrelevant, often inexcusable, these practices cry out for redress. In these and other books of this genre, the children are shown to be victims of a cruel system that eats away at their confidence and fails to meet their needs. Is it the children who are failing in this situation? That is what the grading system would suggest.

Changing Student Expectations

How can these schools stop humiliating the children they are supposed to be teaching? How can they teach these children to expect success in school? First of all, we have to end our preoccupation with disabilities. We know the litany: "Their vocabulary is limited, they cannot think in abstractions, they are not introspective, they prefer physical to mental activity, they lack motivation to succeed in school. . . ." Instead of always trying to "compensate" for disabilities, let us identify, develop, and build on their strengths. In the December 1968 issue of *Grade Teacher* we can read a number of testimonials from teachers who work in the inner city and in isolated rural areas, teachers who are discovering the vast learning potential of their charges. The running theme of these success

---

4. Kenneth B. Clark, "Answer for 'Disadvantaged' Is Effective Teaching," *New York Times*, January 12, 1970. Clark argues as follows:

When one examines the various compensatory or enrichment programs which have been successful in raising the academic achievement of minority-group students, one finds that the significant new ingredient is invariably more effective teaching. It follows, therefore, that the answer to the questions of the best way to teach "the disadvantaged" is embarrassingly simple — namely, to teach them with the same expectations, the same acceptance of their humanity and educability, and, therefore, with the same effectiveness as one would teach the more privileged child. If, on the other hand, one approaches minority-group children with elaborate theories whose rationale is that they cannot or will not learn, the results will be negative. Children are sensitive to all such condescension and they will seek to escape the inherent humiliation of the school experience by various devices — by refusing to learn, by apathy, by aggressive acts, or by unconscious forms of retaliation.

stories is that the teachers did away with all of the negative things they had heard about the "disadvantaged" child. They began with an unshakable belief in the youngsters, a belief soon sustained by pupil achievement. As one teacher said: "I'm fed up with people who keep saying the disadvantaged child can't learn. My children *do* have the ability to learn. They have innate talents just like other children do. If those talents have been smothered by economic, social, and cultural deprivation, it's the teacher's job to discover and nurture them."[5]

Changing Public Expectations

This teacher, along with an increasing number of others, believes that the school has a responsibility not merely to expose each student to a course of instruction, but to give them a real chance to succeed. The same distinction is made by David L. Kirp, a lawyer writing in the *Harvard Educational Review:*[6]

> In the past, schools have not been required to bring about achievement; they have long been thought of as "relatively passive . . . expected to provide a set of free public resources." Yet, the [Supreme] Court has recognized that the state does not satisfy its consitutional responsibility if it merely takes people as it finds them, setting equal standards of access. The state must assure each citizen an effective utilization of the fundamental right. . . . This "effective utilization" standard varies with the different rights: the state is obliged . . . to secure an equal chance for an equal educational outcome.

Like many of the concepts discussed by constitutional lawyers, the standard of effective utilization is deliberately vague as well as challenging. It points in a direction and names a goal but leaves the details for further negotiation. Ultimately, though, we are sure that a citizen has been able to use a right only when he has obtained whatever that right is designed to guarantee.

In the case of basic skills such as reading, to which every citizen has a right, we know that the school has made possible an effective utilization of this right only when its students demonstrate their ability to read. If certain students fail a test, a school might argue that it had done everything humanly possible to teach those students, but the burden of proof should henceforth fall on the school

---

5. "Top Teachers of the Disadvantaged," *Grade Teacher*, December 1968, page 44.

6. David L. Kirp, "The Poor, The Schools, and Equal Protection," *Harvard Educational Review*, Fall 1968, page 652.

and not, as it now does, on the failing student. Moreover, the school should have to show not only that it provided the failing student with instruction that worked with other students who were in some way similar, but that *no* program it could reasonably provide would offer substantial promise of teaching that particular student how to read. In order to argue the latter point, a school official would have to acquaint himself with new and experimental programs that are often widely ignored.

The point of this approach, of course, is not to elicit a whole new set of ingenious arguments about the alleged ineducability of many children. The point is rather to serve clear notice on the schools that society expects *all* its children to learn at least the basic skills, that failures are to be regarded less as the fault of the child or of his background than of the school, and that the proper response to failure (as principals are fond of telling miscreants) is not excuses but reform, and in this case reform by the schools.

Accounting for Competence As Well As for Cash

It would be unfair and also unproductive to lay such a burden on the schools unless we also gave them the means to fulfill these expectations. Increasingly the public is demanding that school officials guarantee the acquisition of basic skills and account for public money spent in terms of certified educational results. How can school officials, already hard-pressed in many areas, meet these demands? What they need is a process of educational engineering through which the schools can obtain a workable technology of instruction. The word *technology* refers not only to devices such as TV cameras, teaching machines, tape recorders, or computer terminals (each of which can help us in certain applications), but more generally to the whole way we go about teaching, the way in which we apply knowledge about education.

How can the process called educational engineering improve the school as it is actually experienced by the students? Of what elements and stages does it consist? What must school officials do in order to make use of educational engineering? In the rest of the chapter we will take up these and other questions in a general way, and then in chapters three, four, and five we will consider in turn each of the main elements of educational engineering.

The principle of public accountability is the key to the adoption of educational engineering, for in order to answer to the public in terms of results, school officials will have to adopt certain managerial procedures that both stimulate the demand for performance and help them provide it. We start with the simple long-established notion that the public has a right to know what benefits they are receiving for their tax dollars. In the field of education the public has so far generally been told or has been able to find out what resources were being purchased, such as personnel, space, and materials. Now, however, the public is beginning to demand that schools extend this principle, and answer in terms not only of how they spend the funds but also of what educational gains they achieve.

This sounds simple enough, but schools must change in several respects in order for the public to know the actual results of instructional programs. First, they have to abandon the traditional practice of withholding all but the most general information on educational accomplishment. This withholding serves interests within the school bureaucracy, but not the interests of the public or of students. A superintendent might worry lest his district fall below the national average, or the average for similar districts, or for districts in his state. A principal might worry lest his school fail to do as well as others in the district, and a teacher lest his class earn lower scores than some other class. People afraid of change might want to suppress data showing that a certain new method or program produces better results than the old ones, that schools in certain areas lag shockingly behind others in their educational results, or that a special program designed and run by a private firm is doing what a school had failed to do. Once the wall of secrecy is broken and public scrutiny begins, the schools, too, will have to act on what their data show; no longer can they simply file the disconcerting reports.

As soon as data currently gathered by the schools is made available, however, public commentators will observe how little the school officials really know about the system they administer. In some of the more advanced systems, officials alert to the problem have begun to collect more useful and reliable information on educational accomplishment, but in many districts, including many of our large metropolitan districts, officials rely on such crude indicators as grade averages, dropout rates and, possibly, a few simple tests. In other words, what the public would discover, if it had the facts now known to school officials, is that officials need to know much more. With the data now generally available, how can they even decide whether a given program has been successful?

In order to evaluate a program, one needs to define in advance exactly what that program is designed to accomplish and how the results will be tested. In place of loosely formulated statements of purpose or inflated curricular ambitions, we need to specify performance criteria that students should be able to meet. In other words, we must go through the discipline of stating goals in terms of what we want the student to be able to *do* at the end of the program. In this sense, the framing of goals and the creation of a corresponding test are closely related.

Who should administer the test and, in broader terms, assess the results of the program? Ordinarily this is done by school personnel, often by those who run the program. Without casting any doubt on the competence or integrity of such personnel, we can observe that in few other fields do we accept unchecked self-assessment quite so casually as in public education. In financial affairs we call in the auditor; in a court case, witnesses; in science, an independent experimenter. The time has come to apply a similar principle in assessing educational accomplishment. When the schools are able to call in an outside auditor of accomplishment, the public will feel assured that a searching, impartial, and reliable assessment will be made.[7]

In short, accountability requires that the school take three steps, each of them a novelty in most school districts: (1) frame performance criteria for each program, (2) obtain an independent educational accomplishment audit to measure the actual performance against these criteria, and (3) provide for the auditor to make a public report of his findings. What accountability means is that members of the public as well as school officials will be able to compare the costs of producing certain benefits in various ways.

The immediate tangible outcome of accountability as outlined above is nothing more than a report with tables and text. In itself, the report has no legal force. It is simply data. It offers no new program. In its broader implications, however, accountability can prepare the way for and support the process of educational engineering. Once we have thorough, relevant, and reliable data on programs of instruction, we naturally raise questions about how

---

7. This is described in more detail in chapter five.

we can increase their effectiveness or lower their cost, or possibly both. And with experience in framing performance criteria, we naturally wonder about revising or extending our educational goals.

In the process of educational engineering we consider these questions not in vague, global terms, but point by point. If a machine malfunctions, engineers immediately look for specific causes. They test the variables, the performance of each part of the assembly, to find out what is going wrong. Rather than reject the machine, question the capability of its operators, or condemn the factory system of production, they go straight to the specific question of what is wrong with the machine.

We can apply a similar approach to education. Instead of blaming the learners, the teachers, their environments, the school system or various parts of it, we can learn to define carefully the performance we want to isolate and the factors that seem to be causing the difficulty, and assure quality by a series of specific changes instead of half-launching or talking to death one grand program after another.

Getting Outside Help

The more specific the change, the less difficult it is to introduce, but very little useful change can come about unless the school has (1) money set aside for that purpose and (2) the management skills needed for innovation within a complex system. Where are these funds or skills to be found? In most school districts all of the money available, especially in a period of war inflation, is needed for routine operating expenses; and officials, especially in the inner city, must spend all their time patching up the present system in order to prevent a breakdown. In fact, where the need for change is greatest, the provision for it seems almost nil. The practice of accountability may show how badly these schools are doing, and may finally arouse a concerted demand for change, but how can the change be managed?

Educational engineering can provide three additional forms of help that, like the accomplishment audit, come from outside the school system and are designed to help the local system, within limits, on its own terms. In other words, the control remains local, but the services are drawn from many sources. In order to draw on the technology of instruction now being developed and to assure that local uses of it are skillful, prudent, thorough, and prompt, a school district needs help in the form of (1) *development or "venture" capital*, earmarked for innovation, supplied in part from federal funds, and set aside from the ordinary operating budget; (2) an outside *management support group* that serves the local board both as a catalyst for the new programs and as a buffer between the board and the groups, agencies, and firms involved in the process of change; and (3) *firms in the knowledge industry* or nonprofit groups that can meet the instructional needs specified by the school board, draw up detailed proposals and bids for doing so, and guarantee to meet the performance criteria set forth in the contract. As noted above, the resulting program is later assessed by (4) an *independent accomplishment auditor* who makes a public report.

These various forms of outside help share three features. They are each independent of the others and of the local school system. In seeking each kind of help, the local board decides which sources of that help to draw upon: which kinds of funds to apply for, which long-term management consultant to retain, which contractors to hire, which auditors to engage. Everything remains under local control. And each form of outside help serves as a complement to the normal school program, not as a replacement for it. For example, development capital stands in addition to the operating budget, and outside personnel engaged for specific purposes work alongside the permanent staff, not above them and not in their place. In fact, many new programs developed and introduced through educational engineering will undertake to train local personnel while also learning from them, so that the program can be turned over to the local staff as soon as it proves its worth. Although educational engineering is a continuing process, applied to a variety of programs, the outside helpers associated with any single program come to "install" that program, not to operate it permanently.

School systems are better at running programs than at starting them. Educational engineering, however, allows them to start programs with no disruption to the operating budget or to staffing patterns. It allows them to draw on a rich variety of talent, in several fields, from anywhere in the country. It provides a way for taking over programs that meet local needs and for ending any failures without stepping on local toes. Along with this low risk, the process offers a possibility of high, even dramatic, gains. Imagine what an energetic and imaginative school district might be able to do when they can call on all the resources we have outlined, resources now often out of their reach. Instead of having to provide every new service from within, as if nobody else had anything to offer, school officials can begin to contract for whatever outside services they need, in the manner familiar to managers of any other complex enterprise. Instead of making impossible, inappropriate, or inefficient demands on the regular staff, they can go to experts in the special services necessary for low-risk, high-gain innovation.

The Performance Contract

In addition to public accountability and the use of outside agencies by the local school system, educational engineering depends on a legal device, the performance contract. Long proven in other areas, this type of contract consists of an agreement not only for services to be rendered but for results to be achieved. In the field of aircraft-engine design, a performance contract would specify not only that engineers do all the calculations and draw all the blueprints, but also that the engine, as built, should produce a certain thrust, consume only so much fuel, tolerate various strains, and so forth. In other words, the engine would have to meet performance criteria. If it failed to do so, the whole process of design and construction would be of little value. In the field of education for basic skills, we can specify that after a given program children be able to do certain things, such as earning a minimum score on a standardized test. Like the engine builder, the educational contractor is bound to meet the established criteria.

What happens if the criteria are not met? Within the flexibility of the contracting process, the parties can agree on any of several kinds of penalties and incentives. For example, the school can provide, and the outside agency agree, that if the students fail to perform as promised, the agency will continue to instruct them, for no additional charge, until they *can* perform; or that for each child who falls short at the end of the program, the agency will forfeit a certain percentage of its fee. The contract might also provide that for each child who exceeds the required gain in performance, the school will pay the agency a certain bonus, depending on the extent of the gain. In fact, the school can demand as much as a reputable contractor, in competition with others, will agree to.

A Process of Educational Engineering: Seven Steps

Now that we have introduced the elements of educational engineering, let us briefly outline the process before examining it in more detail in chapters three, four, and five, and giving an example of the process at work in chapter six. There are seven steps leading up to the actual start of a new educational program:

(1) The local educational authority (LEA) obtains development capital from the Office of Education or another federal agency, the state government, its own local board, or possibly a foundation. Compared with the ordinary operating budget, the amount needed is very small, but at present most officials have no funds at all for development. Whereas energetic firms often devote three to fifteen percent of their budgets to research and development, most school officials would be delighted, as a start, to have as little as one percent set aside strictly for development of new programs.

(2) The LEA next retains a management support group (MSG) whose members have the special skills and experience to assist local officials, as long-term consultants, in dealing with political, social, economic, and educational questions raised by the program being developed. In addition to advising local officials, the MSG can act as a go-between in negotiations with the source of development capital and other outside parties. The LEA, however, retains control over all phases of the operation.

(3) Working with the school staff, the community, and with various groups as required by the situation, the MSG produces a request for proposal (RFP), which is a set of specifications setting forth as clearly as possible the services to be performed, the approximate amount of money to be invested, the restrictions to be observed, the standards to be met, and so forth. The RFP is basically a local blueprint for meeting urgent educational needs.

(4) In the next stage of the educational engineering process, the RFP is sent out to bid. Firms and non-profit agencies that show an interest are invited to a local pre-bidding conference (PBC). Here a rich and varied communication occurs between elements of the private and public sectors. The bidding process allows flexibility to the extent that local officials, with the advice of the MSG, can adopt suggestions made at the PBC.

(5) After suitable revisions, a final RFP is issued and bids are entertained. From these proposals, the LEA selects the ones that seem most promising and invites each of these leading bidders to

present his proposal in more detail, to present a demonstration or exhibit, and to answer questions about it. In short, the process is very similar to what the board would do if it were retaining an architect.

(6) After deliberation the LEA selects what it considers to be the best bid and, with the help of the MSG, enters into negotiation for a performance contract with the successful firm or agency.

(7) While the legal document is being drawn up, the LEA engages an independent educational accomplishment auditor (IEAA) both to monitor execution of the performance contract and to assess the actual results upon which payment to the contractor will depend. Once exactly how the results will be measured is agreed on, the IEAA pretests the children who are to be enrolled in the program and presents the initial scores to the LEA and the contractor. Once that is done, the program itself begins.

Educational engineering, as outlined above, imposes clearly defined requirements but allows for a wide variety of methods. In a sense, this represents a reversal of ordinary conditions, in which the requirements are so loose as to say nothing and the methods so restricted as to allow for little. Although the word *engineering* may at first startle teachers who feel a deep human concern for children, the process we outline can lead to a symbiosis of technology and humanism, wedding the skill of the one to the values of the other. In many schools that now employ a bumbling, primitive technology of instruction, children are repeatedly humiliated because they are not learning what they need to know, and in order to deflect blame from themselves, the staff, as we have said, may blame individual children, or the whole group, or the world from which they come. Where is humanism when we allow children to move down a spiral of failure and self-contempt?

Engineering for Capability in the Public Schools

Educational engineering starts with the assumption that these children *can* succeed, that with an adequate technology of instruction we can lead them toward mastery and a certified sense of accomplishment. What we offer is not another grand manifesto, but a process through which the schools can find programs that work, introduce them, and determine the results. The end product is not a program or a machine or a report, but rather a capability — as, for example, a child's ability to read, *and* the gleam in his eye.

Development Capital for the Schools

Chapter 3

OW CAN AN INSTITUTION renew itself or develop unless
money is set aside for this purpose? In budgeting for any
enterprise, including a school system, we can distinguish
between several kinds of money, such as the operating fund for
routine expenditures, reserve funds, and what businessmen call
venture capital. The first kind of money, familiar to all of us, is
spent in various ways, such as for salaries, supplies, interest on
borrowed money, or any of the other routine expenses that appear on a line-item budget. The second is used for emergencies,
land acquisition, and the like. Venture capital, however, is set
aside strictly for the development of new programs. No firm, except in a stagnant industry, could survive unless it were assured
a supply of this special kind of money. The main reason that our
school systems develop so slowly, so unsurely, is that very few of
their budgets provide any venture capital: no matter how much is
spent per student per year, all of it, or very nearly all, goes for ordinary operating expenses, primarily salaries. Thus school officials
have nothing left over specifically for purposes of change. Is it
any wonder that the capabilities of public education often lag
behind the demands placed on them?

The Need for Development Capital

Many firms, as we have already said, devote from three to fifteen
percent of their budgets to research and development. If as little
as one percent of an education budget were set aside as development capital, we would multiply the initiatives now open to school
officials for improving education. When all of the budget is committed year after year to existing programs, officials have no substantial way to encourage innovations or to support them, and as a
result the system stagnates. People within it may continue to have
new ideas, but how can these ideas ever go further than the endless reports now "filed for further study"? The problem is not

41

necessarily that officials are afraid of change, or would not know how to manage it, but rather that they lack the resources to initiate and sustain it. And when change seems impossible, many of the resourceful, energetic people may leave a system, or grow cynical and bitter as they stay. Thus even the spring of ideas for change may run dry.

When schools fail to do their job, officials usually complain that funds are insufficient; and often they are right. Prices often rise faster than school budgets, and meanwhile some schools are faced with increasingly difficult assignments. When children are not effectively taught basic skills, many taxpayers, asked then to pay for compensatory programs, wonder why the schools could not do their job right the first time around; and when compensatory programs are unable to show satisfactory results either, we may feel that the situation is hopeless and that we may as well not throw good money after bad. In this situation school officials often encounter a scepticism mixed with some despair when they ask for bigger budgets. The sad part is that even if the school board (or in Washington, the Congress) *does* vote more money, the school still lacks what it needs to develop new programs. All it can do is prop up the old ones. What it needs, of course, is development capital.

Until this type of money is available to the schools, they will lack the means to find better ways of doing their job. Present patterns of funding actually encourage officials to tinker endlessly with worn-out programs instead of replacing them with efficient, up-to-date methods. Federal funding, despite a plethora of regulations, guidelines, proposals, and reports, often has the unintentional effect of sustaining inefficiency and inequity in public schools. At all levels of financial support, money is usually directed toward specific problems as they emerge and can no longer be ignored; with few exceptions, it has not been used for an orderly, systematic reform of the education system. Hence, taxpayers face a tragic choice between abandoning hope for certain aspects of the system, and paying a very high price in order to patch up weak schools sufficiently to keep them going.

Using Development Capital Efficiently

The hard lesson to be learned from the past five years of major federal funding of educational programs is that the *kind* of funds is no less important than the *amount*. In order to break the cycle of costly chronic failure in certain schools, political authorities must begin to appropriate discretionary funds not only for successful programs, but also for the renewal of the local school systems. As Daniel Moynihan has rightly said, "The federal government must develop and put into practice far more effective incentive systems than now exist whereby state and local governments, and private interests, too, can be led to achieve the goals of federal programs."[1]

Properly conceptualized, therefore, federal aid to education should be viewed as capital that, when made available in a predictable and systematic way, will provide the energy for educational engineering. Instead of trying to run everything from Washington, we should make it possible for state and local agencies to reexamine and modernize their educational systems. We must do so not simply by distributing additional funds that they can use as they like in the routine operation of a school, but by making available, for the first time on a large scale, a new *type* of support: development capital.

Extending the Scope of Self-Renewal
Once they have a supply of development capital, what can local school officials do that they cannot do now? When discretionary funds become available in a public bureaucracy, each of its bureaus, offices, or agencies can usually be counted on to argue the urgency of its need for more funds and the marvels it will perform if granted its share. In normal practice, discretionary funds can thus disappear rapidly into the enlargement, or extension, or disguised reincarnation of traditional programs. Nothing really changes. If the funds were earmarked for development, however, top officials would be able, with the support of the grantor, to deflect all routine demands. They would be freed to call on outside help to supplement whatever internal initiatives are called forth by the availability of funds. They could start experimental programs without disrupting established ones, and when new programs were proven in practice, they could shift ordinary operating resources on the basis of hard data and local experience. In other words, development capital would allow a school system to discover workable programs on an experimental basis and to adopt them on a large scale within the format of the normal operating

1. Daniel P. Moynihan, "Toward a National Urban Policy," *Public Interest*, Fall 1969, page 16.

budget. At that point, officials could devote the development budget to a new set of problems, extending the scope of self-renewal.

Why do our schools now lack this process of self-renewal? In its recent distinguished report on the schools, the Committee for Economic Development revealed that *much less than one percent* of our total national education investment goes into research and development. On the local level, of course, the percentage is even smaller. "No major industry," the report observes, "would expect to progress satisfactorily unless it invested many times that amount in research and development."[2] Our failure to provide development capital for schools is a very costly saving, the same kind of false economy that might send a firm into bankruptcy. In contrast, if we allow the schools a chance at meaningful development, it is possible that the cost of producing a given unit of educational accomplishment, as independently assessed, might actually *decline* relative to other prices within our economy. In that case, we might still wish to devote the same or even a somewhat higher percentage of our national income to education, but we could expect to receive a substantial increase in effective services from the system. This would be very big news after a period such as the present, in which some parts of the educational system are collapsing even as they absorb a greater share of public resources.

In the absence of development capital, our school systems are too often characterized by archaic budgeting methods; poor use of buildings, staff, and equipment; low salaries; salaries unrelated to performance; inadequate development of personnel; outmoded organization; inadequate teaching materials; primitive technology (in the narrow sense) and, as a result, instructional programs that are often repetitive, uninspired, and clearly ineffective. Until these schools have funds for the development, testing, and installation of new products and practices, the gap between the demand for high-quality education and the performance of the schools will widen even further.

Until the passage of the Vocational Education Act of 1963 and the Elementary and Secondary Education Act of 1965, there was virtually no money earmarked for this general purpose in education. Of the funds made available by this legislation, only a very

2. Committee for Economic Development, *Innovation in Education: New Directions for the American School*, Summer 1968, page 29.

small percentage went for development capital, about three dollars out of every thousand; but the principle was established. In 1968 the superintendent of schools in Dallas obtained a one-cent tax increase as a set-aside for use as development capital. Recently the National School Boards Association passed a resolution urging that the federal government supply local boards with a two and one-half percent set-aside, a very modest figure compared with standard practice in many business enterprises. When the benefits of development capital become as apparent in education as they are elsewhere, we should not be surprised to find legislatures and boards willing to set aside a more appropriate amount — three percent for purposes of systematic self-renewal.

Development Capital and Accountability

In confronting the problems of our most severely challenged schools, however, the people who establish budgets have so far provided severely restricted percentages of development capital, and have left most programs, and most school districts, with none at all. Why have they failed to move faster? First, the idea of developmental allocations has been applied to education for only a few years, and many officials are too busy struggling to pay operating costs to indulge the hope of a discretionary fund that they could use actually to improve the system. Second, some people feel that educational bureaucracies have done so badly in some areas that they might squander discretionary funds or not know what to do with them. In educational engineering, however, school organizations are not expected to work miracles unassisted; they are given ways to call on a variety of outside help, including not only funds, as before, but management support, actual program operation, and accomplishment auditing. Third, legislators may hesitate to give money for a purpose as vague as "development" — after all, how are they supposed to judge whether the money is wisely spent?

This question leads us into the relation between development capital and accountability. For as long as the schools are not answerable to their source of funds in terms of demonstrable results produced, then the charge of vagueness remains. In contrast, if we adopt the process of accountability (as outlined in chapter two and explained more fully in chapter five), then we can justify our use of development capital, for we will have the certified results to show. In fact, the relation between these two concepts really runs both ways. Without development capital, accountability would be unfair: how can we hold a manager answerable for results if we deprive him of the means required to produce them? Conversely, as soon as we entrust an educational manager with discretionary funds, we can properly insist that he structure programs in such a way as to show what educational accomplishment they produce.

Sources of Development Capital

Once the advantages of this procedure are recognized, where are the schools going to get the necessary funds? Apart from foundations and other private sources, development capital must come largely from two sources: the school system itself, through its ordinary source of funds, and higher levels of government, primarily the federal level. In the case of local funds, the board can simply set aside a percentage of the budget or, where the budget is being enlarged, specify additional funds as development capital. When local districts develop programs that might appeal to other districts, they can also earn a kind of non-profit income in return for helping others install their programs; this money can then be plowed back into the development fund. Also, when new programs succeed in producing a given unit of educational accomplishment for less than the old program cost, all or part of the saving might be applied to further development, as in other successful enterprises.

Some funds at the federal level should be applied to high-risk investments, at least in part, for this is the only level of government that can ordinarily afford to commit large sums to basic research and development, as in President Nixon's call for a national institute of education. In addition, the federal government should support a continuing search for successful practices around the nation, both in school management and in classroom methods. Finally, in accordance with the concept sometimes called the new federalism, the federal government should provide development capital for education directly to local boards as well as to state agencies.

In making direct grants, the federal government has faced many quandries, and among them are the difficulty in obtaining thorough, reliable reports on what effect a program has produced, and the tendency of school districts that are already well off to write better applications and thus get even richer while needy districts get less than their share of the funds. Both of these difficulties can be surmounted through the process of educational engineering — in particular, through a three-stage funding of projects.

The Three Stages of Project Funding

In this process of funding, the first stage provides for planning grants, small amounts of money that enable the school district to retain a management support group or other technical assistance. With the help of this outside advice and expertise, the local district can work out a sophisticated, relevant, and imaginative program. Since every district will have access to expert help, the more advanced districts will lose their unfair advantage in applying and the districts that need most help will develop much better ideas on how to use the federal money available.

The second stage of funding is the awarding of program grants to those schools that, with the help of the planning grants, have evolved the most promising programs. Has the school assessed its own needs in a plausible way? Has it worked out a program that, if successful, would meet those needs? Finally, does the program specify clear performance criteria by which we can judge success? All of these questions can be answered on the basis of the "request for performance" prepared by the school for potential bidders. The art in writing an RFP is to set the parameters so the bidders can respond to the school's real needs.

Once the RFP is reviewed and approved by the granting agency and the grant is made, the local district has one more task before the program is complete enough to begin operation. In this third stage of funding, which follows automatically upon the second, the granting agency requires that the local district engage an independent educational accomplishment auditor. In the cycle of educational engineering, the auditor enters after the program is planned so that he feels no interest in its success, and before its operation actually begins so that he can pretest the students. Appropriately trained and certified, the IEAA is directly employed neither by the federal government nor by the local district, but rather by a private firm, a university center, or a non-profit organization. Ultimately, he is responsible to the public, not to any government agency, but his reports obviously assist officials at all levels of government in deciding on future applications. Once the standards of measurement are agreed upon and the pretest made, the granting agency releases the money already committed in the second stage of funding, and the program begins.

What we have described is one pattern of grants management, an element in the larger process of educational engineering. When federal funds are distributed uniformly, say a certain amount per registered student, grants management is superfluous except in the most mechanical sense of counting heads and disbursing funds. However, when the federal government seeks to use part of its education money to stimulate and support innovation in local schools (as well as in research locations), we do need a flexible, sensitive method for assuring that the funds are in fact used for development, not diverted into sustaining the structure that they are intended to change.

Keeping the Money Flow Effective

Perhaps only a person who has worked in a large bureaucracy can appreciate the variety of ingenious devices by which money intended for development can be used to prop up the programs most in need of replacement. Why does this occur? It occurs because existing programs, no matter how inept, irrelevant, or even harmful, always need more money; and the less successful a program becomes, the more money it quite naturally needs. Or to view this problem the other way around, new programs or ideas are often primarily sponsored not by an established and powerful group within a system, but by relatively young people, by outside consultants, or by others who lack significant power. Their ideas may win the approval of leadership, especially if the proposal seems likely to elicit a grant, but when the money is dispensed, much of it may flow, again quite naturally, into the more established channels. When this happens, development capital is depreciated into the common status of operating money; it loses any power to support innovation. Instead it can only preserve the local programs whose failure had stimulated the granting of development capital.

In fact, federal programs designed to initiate change can produce a bureaucratic expansion not only in Washington but also in each of the states and in many of the local districts.[3] Gradually, the people involved may come to think less in terms of the educational

3. According to a survey of progress within a major federal education program, "resistance within the established bureaucracies of large-city school systems appears to have cut into the effectiveness of some Title I programs." In Detroit, for example, the director of these programs said that "the biggest thorn in our side is our own organization. Change is coming very hard. . . . Many teachers and administrators battle us daily." ("Federal Education Aid to Poor Is Found to Have Little Effect," *New York Times*, December 28, 1969, p. 48.)

results originally sought by the legislation than in terms of the maintenance of the structure created to administer the funds. What began as an effort to support certain kinds of innovation can thus become yet another vested bureaucratic interest. How can this degeneration be avoided?

Defining and Using Development Capital

Finding answers to this question is one of the most challenging tasks facing students of organizations and government. There are no magic solutions. We might begin, however, by distinguishing development capital very sharply from ordinary grants and operating funds. In order to make the difference unmistakable, we could even say that development capital is money used in opposition to prevailing practices, or money used for creating alternatives to something that is being done. Its use implies a judgment, if not that things are bad, at least that they could be significantly better. Development capital thus deliberately induces tension within the system, as does any effort to find better methods. Perhaps we can define development capital most clearly by saying frankly that its purpose is to oust (and of course, to replace) a failing or sluggish part of the system. Thus, in applying for development capital, applicants should be prepared to say what they would like to get rid of.

In this sense, development capital makes possible a productive form of competition based on the belief that no system can flourish unless it is exploring more than one way of doing things. When substantive change seems impossible in a bureaucracy, competition is restricted to empire-building and other forms of non-productive labor. In educational engineering, we seek to convert the inevitable competition into substantive achievements, such as finding better ways to teach reading. We do so by supporting various ad hoc developmental units within local districts, units that deliberately reject the conventional wisdom of the system they serve, that explicitly question or even oppose certain practices within the system, and that, in effect, seek to produce a shake-up within their particular sphere.

Why should any system wish to harbor such a unit? For some of the same reasons that we support civil liberties: so that we are not cut off from the sources of change, even when the ideas may not at first please us; so that we are saved from a single, impoverished notion of reality; so that we may grow and develop. In this sense, a grant of development capital ought to serve the same function as the words of a loyal opposition, a source of alternatives. Each assumes we can do better.

In education, however, funds intended to support a loyal opposition have usually been either allied with all other resources, local, state, and federal, as part of the operating budget, or used to create programs to supplement the regular program. Online programs, research activities, and federally funded innovative programs, as well as all other programs covered by the Elementary and Secondary Education Act, are incompatibly lumped together in the total program. In order to sustain a process of educational engineering, this practice must be sharply altered. We must clearly distinguish among funds for the continuation of existing programs, for the local installation of new but validated programs, and for the development and testing of innovations.

Once this distinction is established we can generally allocate these three functions among the various levels of government.[4] Thus it seems appropriate that existing local programs be supported by taxes raised within the district and by additional operating expense funds that the state may supply. In contrast, the state might well support local adoptions of newly developed and validated programs. Such incentive grants to districts will enable them to initiate new programs without having to place the relatively high installation cost directly on the taxpayers of the local district. Finally, federal funds for education ought to be allocated for the development and testing of new programs that local districts, with the help of state funds, can install and henceforth support as part of their regular operating budgets. Federal funds would thus be granted in the form of performance contracts to universities, state departments of education, and private industry, as well as to local districts that have the ideas and capacity for developing new programs. In general, however, federal discretionary funds would not be given to local districts for the routine support of traditional or newly adopted instructional programs.

In summary, according to this division of labor in the pattern of funding, the federal government would provide nearly all the support for educational development, although the actual work

---

4. The outline of this and the following paragraphs represents discussions among the author, Dr. Karl Hereford, and Dr. Edward A. Welling, Jr.

would be done not only by national institutes, but by state departments, local districts, university centers, and even private firms. State governments, while continuing to provide a portion of the routine funds of the various local districts, would direct substantial funds for helping schools meet the high one-time installation costs for new programs that had been developed and tested with federal money. And the local districts, as always, would raise the ordinary operating funds from local taxes and from normal state supplements. In addition the local school budgets would sometimes include, within separate categories, development grants from federal sources and installation grants from the state.

Competition for Alternatives

Earlier in this chapter we outlined a three-stage funding process for the development of new educational programs. Now we can see that development itself is only one of three stages in the process of educational engineering. After we design and test the model for a new program, local schools must install it and then sustain its regular use (at least until they can replace it with something even better). Educational engineering requires that funds intended for each of these three stages be kept separate within local school budgets; and that basic support for each stage be assigned to an appropriate level of government, so that broad decisions about development gain from the national perspective, programs for installation respond to state plans, and the adoption and management of new programs be thoroughly decentralized and kept close to the people they serve.

The use of development or venture capital implies competition. In the world of business, an investment banker must decide which of several firms offers the best prospects; and for each of the firms, which of its own programs to support; and for each of the programs, which managers to assign and subcontractors to hire. In each case, various groups compete. With appropriate modifications, we can profit from the use of similar incentives in the field of education. The process of educational engineering offers several points at which a variety of groups are invited to show what each of them can offer, and funds are shared according to what is shown. For example, (1) in awarding grants for the development of new programs, the federal government might weigh need rather heavily in the distribution of planning grants, so that relatively weak local districts could obtain help from management support groups in the writing of final applications; but once the applications were submitted, the granting agency would choose among them on the basis of quality alone. Similarly, (2) when a local district prepares to award a performance contract for instructional services, it calls for bids from a wide variety of private firms, non-profit organizations, and even ad hoc groups from within the local system; and (3) when the district chooses between its own way of producing a certain educational accomplishment and one or more new ways, it is once again involved in a kind of competition. The point, of course, is not to set people against one another, but to use incentives to call forth useful alternatives. Otherwise, managers have nothing to choose among, and are reduced to patching up whatever they started with.

All three forms of competition listed above share one important feature: they all occur within our system of public education and are designed to strengthen it, especially in areas where its achievement now is low. Some critics of the public schools are urging other forms of competition that might pit private enterprise *against* the public schools instead of putting it to work, as we propose, on their behalf. Nonetheless, for as long as public schools fail to make full use of educational engineering, we may need to put development capital in the hands not of school officials but of individual parents. In chapter one we mentioned the voucher plans now being developed. Some of them have very broad ranges, proposing virtually complete public support through voucher for a variety of otherwise private schools. Apart from broad schemes, however, the voucher mechanism might help us in providing particular kinds of education on a trial basis for certain groups of students, especially compensatory education for "disadvantaged" students who need to learn basic skills and are not being helped by the public schools.

A Voucher System

One scheme might work as follows: for each student in need of compensatory education, the school system sets aside an adequate amount of money in an escrow account. This money is held for payment to suppliers of educational service, and may neither be withdrawn by the school system nor collected by the supplier until he meets performance criteria. Parents of the designated students receive a voucher representing their shares of the escrow account. The parents of each child may "spend" his voucher at any educational agency, including a private firm, that will guarantee to produce certain educational results. In place of complaining to an unresponsive public school, the parents can thus send their child, at least for compensatory education, to whatever agency has a reputation for effectiveness.

A limited voucher scheme such as this would share several virtues with the process of educational engineering outlined in this book. First of all, it would attract various kinds of talent and develop various programs of instruction that are now unavailable within, or inaccessible to, the public schools. It would establish a market mechanism under certain controls so that programs could be compared and freely chosen. It would increase the participation of parents and other members of the community in educational decisions. With the voucher in hand, a parent would be able to influence which services are made available and motivated to learn which ones will help his child the most. The scheme would foster accountability, for the supplier of services would not collect his money from the escrow account unless impartial tests showed that his students had reached the agreed level of achievement. Ideally, therefore, such a scheme would lead to accountability, responsiveness, and ingenuity in compensatory education.

In practice, however, a voucher scheme might raise several hard questions: on what basis would the parents of failing students be able to "shop" effectively among the competing claims of public schools, private schools of many kinds, and educational programs run by private firms? To what extent are we willing to surrender our heritage of common public schools for the sake of a free-for-all educational marketplace? Is there not some way for public schools to enlist outside talent for certain purposes and to make its own use of incentive plans?

Incentives and Support for Innovation
Educational engineers believe there *is* a way, based in part on the principle of accountability and the provision of development capital within the school system. Consider a couple of further examples. We could adopt the idea of the escrow account, mentioned above as part of a voucher scheme, and use it instead to provide

incentives inside a public school or district. When a school under-
took a new program, the federal or state government could make
an incentive grant that the granting agency would deposit in an
escrow account rather than give directly to the school. If the school
made the program a success, as measured by an independent
educational accomplishment audit, the incentive grant would be
passed along to the school, which could use it to help pay for the
next round of innovation or for incentive awards to supplement the
basic salaries of participating teachers.

At present, very few teachers receive additional income for
anything except piling up seniority and academic credits in education courses. Typically, the highest salary is approximately twice
the local starting salary, and it is achieved by a combination of
staying on the job for ten years and collecting sixty units of academic credit beyond the B.A. degree. Since formal training of
more than about thirty graduate units (the M.A.) has never been
required for employment in the public schools, we might reform
the salary schedule so as to offer the top salary after thirty units
instead of luring teachers to accumulate sixty. In addition, we
could establish an escrow account for incentive pay based on the
educational results teachers produce. Such a system would not
contain the negative aspects of merit pay, but it *would* provide
strong incentives to achieve self-imposed goals. Thus, rather than
placing an arbitrary ceiling on a teacher's possible income, we
could arrange the incentives so that he is limited only by the degree of his willingness to invest his time, effort, and imagination
in improving the quality of education. Such a system would offer
rewards for the achievement of measurable results as well as for
training and seniority.[5]

School officials can use incentive capital not only for paying bonuses to outstanding teachers, but for supporting programs suggested by members of the staff, of the local community, or of the
student body. People will sometimes work harder to see their own
ideas put to the test than to receive a bonus. How can we enlist the

5. One plan for incentives was outlined by Allen Calvin in "Let's Reward Good Teachers,"
Educational Technology, October 1969, pages 97–98. Where could schools get money for incentives? Arguing that we do not necessarily have to go to the federal government, Calvin notes
that "at the present time we are spending millions of dollars a year for in-service teacher training and staff development," and that since "it has yet to be demonstrated that these monies
contribute anything to increased learning on the part of the student," we might instead "transfer these funds directly to the school systems to be used to reward effective teaching."

surprising amount of energy that people are willing to devote to programs they work out for themselves? In California, the superintendent of a large school district was allowed to manage about one percent of the local operating budget (some $250,000) as an investment account. Board policy also permitted the allocation of discretionary funds raised outside the district from federal, state, and private sources. In the period 1965-68 the board, advised by the superintendent, allocated the investment funds among proposals from teachers, students, and administrators, all of which were in competition with one another for the available funds. In making these investment decisions, the board and the superintendent had the assistance of an elected group of teachers called the Academy of Instruction, and the cooperation of the administrators and community members. No proposal was considered unless it clearly defined its goals.

This local grants-management policy led quickly to significant changes in student accomplishment, teacher effectiveness, and administrator initiative. The district soon had an educational resources center, a zero-reject reading laboratory, a physical fitness testing center, a humanities center, and a vocational education program established within the basic curriculum. Funds were also used for a project in drug education that led to production of a film designed to explain the dangers of LSD and other drugs. This film proved so popular that sales to other school systems earned the district a non-profit income of about $100,000, which was added to the investments account. Apart from its immediate and tangible effects, the modest one percent allocation also served as a "rudder" that soon affected the direction of future operating budgets.[6]

We could give other examples of how development capital can provide incentives and support for innovations in the schools; of how it can summon the energies of individual teachers as well as of local districts and private firms. But we have already outlined the need for, character of, and sources for development capital. We can now discuss the various arrangements through which this special kind of money, once made available, can transform our technology of instruction.

6. This program is further described in "Structuring Teachers Into the Decision Making Process" by Robert Grimes, *Journal of Secondary Education*, December 1969, pages 346-51. Mr. Grimes is a member and past chairman of the Academy of Instruction, San Mateo Union High School District, in California.

Management
Support,
Performance
Contracts,
and the
Technology
of Instruction

Chapter 4

O NCE THE NEW KIND of money is available, how do we put it to work? Its purpose is to improve the technology of instruction, so we ought to begin by considering what that means. Some educators glimpse great promise in the movement suggested by this phrase, while for others it conjures up the dismal image of teachers being replaced by costly, delicate, badly programmed, dehumanizing machines. Undoubtedly schools have found that the educational results of certain machinery have fallen short, sometimes considerably short, of hopes inspired by the salesmen of these products and by some educators who failed to distinguish between the long-range potential of technology and the limited capabilities of the first generation of instructional machinery. This distinction was made clear, for example, by Congressman John Brademas when he urged in 1969 that "we must stop thinking of technology in this country solely as hardware or equipment" and noted that "educational technology goes far beyond equipment to embrace the shaping of the most effective strategies of instruction. . . ."[1]

The Scope of Instructional Technology

In its distinguished report of March 1970, the Commission on Instructional Technology, under the chairmanship of Sterling M. McMurrin, developed this point further, observing that in its more familiar sense, instructional technology means "the media born of the communications revolution which can be used for instructional purposes alongside the teacher, textbook, and blackboard."[2] These media, of course, include television, films, overhead projectors, computers, and other widely used or well-publicized items

1. John Brademas, *Congressional Record*, August 7, 1969, page E6804.

2. This and other quotations in this paragraph are taken from page 19 of *To Improve Learning*, a report by the Commission on Instructional Technology, U.S. Government Printing Office, 1970.

of "hardware" and "software." In nearly every case, says the report, "these media have entered education independently, and still operate more in isolation than in combination." Although the commission reluctantly followed the current restricted usage of the term "instructional technology," it made very clear its hope that we would soon learn to extend our usage of the term "beyond any particular medium or device." The more generous definition they offer is worth a close look:

> In this sense, instructional technology is more than the sum of its parts. It is a systematic way of designing, carrying out, and evaluating the total process of learning and teaching in terms of specific objectives, based on research in human learning and communication, and employing a combination of human and nonhuman resources to bring about more effective instruction. The widespread acceptance and application of this broad definition belongs to the future. Though only a limited number of institutions have attempted to design instruction using such a systematic, comprehensive approach, there is reason to believe that this approach holds the key to the contribution technology can make to the advancement of education.

In the future envisioned by this report, which could be nearer than is generally expected, schools will no longer be left to shop among hundreds of uncoordinated gadgets, many of which now do little more than duplicate questionable teaching practices or provide illustrations. Instead, schools will start with performance criteria, with specifications of what results they want to produce. They will be in the market not for bits and pieces of what we now call technology, but rather for systematic programs designed to produce the desired results. No longer will schools have to base their purchases on the claims of equipment salesmen; they will soon be able to consult verified data on the educational accomplishment produced by each program, under specified conditions.

The Need for Research and Assessment

This day may come sooner than we expect, but before then we must take several big steps in reforming the way the schools are run, and meanwhile we should also bear in mind the cautionary words of Anthony G. Oettinger in his book, *Run, Computer, Run:*

> My aim in analyzing the myths, the institutional failure, the brazen exploitations, the oppressive self-delusions that make a mockery of

technological change in education is not to deny the promise, but to rescue it from unmerited disillusionment. I say there are no easy victories, no quick answers, no panaceas. If we are to realize the promise, we must not allow our human and material resources to be diverted into showy changes in form that will continue to block changes in substance. Fundamental ignorance remains to be overcome in many realms that bear on the successful application of modern technology to education and we must therefore be prepared to encourage long-term investment in the exploration of diverse paths.[3]

In other words, all of us should recognize that there is no magic box that can transform the schools overnight. We need a substantial, continuing program of research that starts not with the machinery we happen to have available now, but with the job to be done; and we also need a mechanism through which local schools can assess the merits and suitability of alternative programs as they are developed, arrange for experts to install the program chosen for a particular purpose, and assign others to measure its actual results.

For the first of these two tasks we need work by a research center within the federal government and by a variety of private firms, university centers, and other non-profit organizations. Like research in medicine or agriculture, this effort will never end because once the process is begun we will continue to find better methods of meeting standard educational needs and new demands as they arise. Research alone, however, leads no further than the laboratory door, the pages of a journal, a demonstration classroom, or perhaps some headlines. How will local schools arrange to install one of these programs? In general, how will good instructional practices spread from a research center to schools that need them?

For this second task we need the process of educational engineering. Schools have long sought help from outside agencies, but they now require new kinds of help and a mechanism for relating them. For years the schools bought hardly any instructional technology more complicated than textbooks and some relatively simple audio-visual equipment. In fact, technology in the schools has so far hardly gone beyond the presence of some TV sets that, though long as familiar to the child as his toys or tricycle, are often

---

3. Anthony G. Oettinger, *Run, Computer, Run* (Harvard University Press, 1969), quoted in the report by the Commission on Instructional Technology, Sterling McMurrin, Chairman, page 20.

regarded with suspicion by teachers and, with few exceptions, used ineffectively. The schools, lacking a process of management through which they could master the available technology, adopt it erratically and use it sloppily. The suppliers, in the absence of specific, informed challenges to make what the schools really need, simply market what they have. How can this wasteful, discouraging pattern be broken?

Speaking to the American Psychological Association in 1968, Henrik Gideonse discussed some of the steps educators must take so that industry can respond successfully to the need for programs more sophisticated and flexible than the common textbook. In closing he said:

> The assessment of output, the incorporation of accountability, and the development of strategies and tactics of resource control constitute the necessary precondition for the effective involvement of industry in the solution of the problems which plague American education today. As management techniques begin to identify the character of the problems confronting schools, then the developmental, inventive, and managerial genius of American industry will find arenas for productive labor and investment in education.[4]

What this means, in part, is that until we can say what we need, we are going to continue being offered gadgets rather than programs of instructional technology; and that until we can obtain a regular, reliable assessment of the results of each program, we will have no way of comparing their cost effectiveness. This calls for a new pattern of managing education.

Look what happened when we appropriated large sums of federal money for education without also developing a process of educational engineering: the discernable results, as seen from the local level, seem curiously fragmentary. Why? The efforts to bring about change seem to have lacked a pervasive and sustaining philosophy of change as a constant, desirable, even necessary condition. They have also lacked a system of sustained logistical support for encouraging and reinforcing the desire and willingness to change. And finally, they have lacked a well-developed concept of management. Together, these shortcomings form a depressingly inconclusive picture of our educational system's ability to cope with change.

4. Hendrik Gideonse, Director, Program Planning and Evaluation, Bureau of Research, U.S. Office of Education, "Industry- Education Relations: A Three Year Appraisal," Speech to the American Psychological Association Convention in San Francisco, September 1, 1968.

Moreover, many of those who recently pioneered in proposing some form of educational change seem to have lacked staying power. What happened to the innovators? Many, perhaps, were victims of their own naiveté. Too few got to know the whole scene, and having welcomed comparative isolation from the frustrations of the gargantuan system, they have since been devoured by or driven from it. These pioneers found that the organizations they tried to work within are structured, in effect, not for innovation but for business as usual. When they sought outside help, they found little, if any.

What were they up against? In general they found themselves hedged in by local constraints, bound by tradition, frustrated by legal binders, stymied by community apathy. They encountered fear on the part of teachers, inflexible personnel policies and practices, "yo-yo" financing, underdeveloped planning capabilities, a staff untrained for adapting to change, a maze of regulations, the debilitating strains of project grantsmanship, and the lack of adequate provisions for calling on the necessary outside help. Armed only with the enthusiasm of innocence, they discovered the realities of institutional inertia. Bright people with bright ideas found themselves thwarted by the machinery, or lack of it, through which ideas in education can be translated into practice. Failing to receive the philosophical, logistical, or management support so necessary to sustain their ideas, many of our innovators allowed the situation to defeat them.

Opening the Closed System

The first lesson we may draw from this dismal experience is that local schools can no longer go it alone. In order to meet new conditions, they need help from the outside as well as innovators on the inside. Until very recently, we have thought of outside assistance mainly in terms of money, especially federal funds. Now we are recognizing that federal funds, no matter how necessary, are far from sufficient. Schools also need outside help in the form of management support and of program development. In place of trying to do everything themselves, they need to forge new alliances and partnerships with various groups that can offer certain managerial and educational services.

The prevailing image in school administration is still the closed system, which, with the occasional advice of various consultants, provides all of the managerial skills, instructional services, and assessment procedures it decides are necessary. The most sophisticated technology that it generally seeks to buy is textbooks, pieces of audio-visual machinery, and some standardized tests. In the field of management (or "administration"), the school seldom receives any help at all. Although the local system is responsive to certain community demands and to trends or fashions within the world of education, it remains essentially closed with respect to its capabilities.

We have seen the results.

School administrators now face the challenge of opening their systems. In the future, an educational manager will gain his reputation not by trying to do everything from within, but rather by calling deftly on a variety of outside services and putting them to work within the schools. He will recognize that for purposes of innovation, certain services are best organized *outside* the public school bureaucracy. The skillful educational manager will see that his job is not singlehandedly to create new programs, but to make good use of the people who do. He will define his role and that of the local community in terms of (1) deciding what results they want, (2) overseeing the process of innovation, and (3) operating new programs once they have been firmly installed within the local system.

What can we expect from the open educational system? First, it will not only assure local control as before but will finally provide the innovative skills that local districts need to meet their goals. It will continue to rely on its internal staff to do what they can do best, but it will no longer expect the staff to enact miracles of reform without adequate outside help. In the process of obtaining various forms of assistance, the open educational system will define its needs precisely and specifically, since it will have to tell somebody outside what *he* should do. It will offer the educational manager a flexibility never before enjoyed: he will ultimately be able, like other managers, to draw on the range of alternative services stimulated by national competition, and to assign special tasks to groups of specialists experienced in a variety of educational settings. In experimenting with new methods, he will be able to discard programs or services that fail to meet his criteria, and to institutionalize only the ones that work.

The Management Support Group

As educational systems begin to open up, what goods and services will they be seeking? In chapter three we discussed their need for development capital. Once it becomes available in significant amounts, probably from the federal government, what help will local schools need to derive the maximum benefits from this new kind of money? First of all, as we have suggested, they need management support. We might go so far as to warn that without management support the development capital would probably be drawn back into the orbit of "business as usual," and thus would fail to produce the development for which it was appropriated. In this case, the capital would be wasted not because the local educational manager opposed change but because he did not have the help he needed in order to bring it about.

How can a management support group assist him? In a nutshell, the MSG should act as a catalyst and a buffer. This concept is new to education. Its precedent was established in the field of defense when, in the mid-1950s, the Aerospace Corporation was created as a buffer and technical assistance team between the Air Force and the suppliers of weapons systems. Its function was to develop programs, design requests for proposals based on performance specifications, assist in evaluating proposals, and provide management services to contractors. (Obviously we are not urging that educators adopt this model exactly; we are simply pointing out that the general need for a buffer group exists no less in the process of educational change than in military procurement.)

Let us consider how a typical management support group can function to support the educational process we are proposing.[5] Retained by the local school district and subject to its direction, the MSG assists in program planning, in evaluating bids, and in project management. School systems generally lack such a management capability or, if they do have a staff for this purpose, it is usually kept busy on day-to-day operations. Moreover, an outside group provides new insights and a different perspective in analyzing educational problems and developing alternative solutions. Members of the MSG have worked in a variety of institutions; undistracted by the pressures of routine school administration,

5. It should be kept in mind that this discussion is *not* theoretical; the method presented has been used in the Texarkana project and elsewhere (see chapters six and seven).

they keep in close touch with developments in their special fields; and they can focus their attention on a specific problem.

The MSG takes part in each step of the following process, described in roughly chronological order: at the start it helps to analyze the educational needs of the community, to set the standards of student performance, and to define the outlines of the eventual program. It advises on sources of funding, a complex task in itself, and one on which outside help can make the difference between success and failure, especially for the overburdened schools that most need money. The MSG develops a *request for proposal* (RFP), a document that will be sent to potential bidders after local discussion, editing, and approval. The group helps the school officials in gathering and maintaining political and community support during all phases of the program. It assists in preparing an experimental design for the evaluation of the program and, assuming the results are good, for its continuing use by the local system and its adoption by others. The MSG talks with potential bidders in the education industry and in development laboratories to ensure that the RFP will call on the full range of newly available methods; and having meanwhile prepared a list of qualified bidders, it sends them the revised RFP. While firms are writing their proposals, the MSG helps the local school board establish a procedure for evaluating them.

Once this initial phase is completed, the school board has before it a variety of proposals in response to the RFP; and when it selects one of these bids, the second phase begins. With the MSG's help, the board negotiates a performance contract with the winning bidder and engages an independent educational accomplishment auditor (IEAA). When he has completed his pretest, the instructional program begins. During the course of the program, the MSG acts as a buffer between the school board and the contractor, evaluating progress and working out the adjustments always required in a complex program. Meanwhile, it analyzes the administrative changes that will be necessary when the program is proven and the school fully takes over its operation. This phase is sometimes called the turnkey phase because, if the whole operation is properly planned, the program should be so thoroughly debugged and so well integrated into the local system that the contractor can, as it were, turn the keys over to local officials and the project can continue without a hitch, using local staff trained by the contractor during the experimental phase. Clearly, planning for the turnkey phase must begin at the very start of the operation, so that local staff are operating the whole program by the time the contract expires.

As an unofficial advocate of change and ombudsman for the public interest, the MSG can provide an effective, disinterested, and politically palatable linkage among federal, state, and local agencies so that priorities mesh, standards are met, and programs are coordinated. Because many firms of unknown or dubious reliability will be entering this newly created multi-billion-dollar market, the MSG is a necessary mediator and honest broker between the firms and the school systems. At the community level, it can also help school officials take into account the vested interests of powerful groups and important decision makers. Acting as a buffer between the school board and these various interest groups, the MSG can sound out positions, obtain information, and propose possible plans in such a way that, if specific ideas are not accepted by the board, the superintendent can point to the group as a scapegoat, thus preserving his flexibility. Finally, it can hire potential school employees so that local officials can see them in action before having to offer them a job, and it can provide access on short notice to consultants around the country without having to go through cumbersome bureaucratic procedures.

So far we have described two forms of outside help to local schools: in chapter three we explained the concept of development capital, and in the first part of this chapter, the concept of management support. Now we may consider in more detail the third source of outside help, the supplier of instructional technology, and the device through which he is harnessed to the specific needs of a school, the performance contract.

The Performance Contract

A performance contract is a legal agreement between a local school board and a supplier of instructional programs providing that the amount and schedule of payment will depend not on what services are said to have been provided, but on the degree of increase in student accomplishment, as independently audited, in the field of the program. In requesting bids for such a contract, the board specifies the results it wants, leaving the various firms to propose what methods they would use. In selecting a firm, the board could, of course, reject any proposal resting on a method that it did not approve of and that in its opinion failed to deal with local conditions adequately. But the method of instruction, after approval by the board and within supervision exercised by the MSG, is the business of the winning firm; and at the conclusion of the program, what the board reviews is not the process of instruction, but the accomplishment of the students, their performance on specified tests. Especially if the students do well, the board will take a keen interest in *how* the results were produced, but in any case the payment will depend on an evaluation of the product, not of the process which led to it.

As we remarked about the new media of instruction, so should we say of performance contracts: they are not a magic solution to all of our problems. When used casually, they may solve nothing at all; and if used wrongly, they could even do harm. For example, a performance contract is appropriate only when the results we desire are measurable. If nobody can reliably measure "maturity," or "good style" in composition, we have no business applying performance contracts to programs that are intended, somewhat vaguely perhaps, to teach these qualities. But the obvious fact that many valuable results of education are loosely defined or ill-suited to quantitative measurement should not deter us from dealing with other results that we *can* specify and assess rather precisely. Some of the most grave failures of our schools occur in fields such as high-school social studies in which the larger goals are virtually impossible to measure on any tests now available. Problems such as this call for solutions other than performance contracts. We can, however, apply performance contracts to the problem of teaching such basic skills as reading and arithmetic. In between these extremes there are questionable areas where they might help but might also distort the program; and in these areas we ought to err now on the side of caution. There is plenty of work to be done on the basic skills, and if performance contracts help us do it, they will have won honor enough.

Benefits of Performance Contracting
Through performance contracts, a school board can introduce a more sophisticated technology of instruction. Undoubtedly this technology will rely in part on various media in addition to the blackboard and textbook. In some cases these new media will take over routine jobs that now distract the teacher from helping individual students with special problems and overburden him with

the less challenging parts of his work. If the new media are successful, they will transform people who are now serving much of the time as instructors into what they want to be: teachers. Nothing in schools is more mechanical and dehumanizing than the dreary, endlessly repetitive routine of instructing too many children in the most basic skills. The technology that we develop ought not to *compete* with teachers; it ought to *free* them to do other things that now are sadly, and necessarily, neglected. In itself, the new technology is not good or bad. Its value depends on the way we use it and, as we have said, on the results it can produce.

So, too, with performance contracting. Properly used, it can facilitate the trial and evaluation of new programs . Many good instructional programs have not been given the opportunity to demonstrate their potential because of the lack of an effective delivery system at the local level. Instead of insisting that we install these programs directly in our regular school curriculum, the educational engineer would propose that we try them first in a separately managed center with its own accounting procedures and operating practices. In this case, the risk is small, and the delivery is relatively simple.

Second, performance contracting for instructional services can introduce greater resources and versatility into our public schools. Right now, new programs are being offered to the public outside the school system: the process of fragmentation has begun. Several large corporations are establishing franchise learning centers across the country. One firm has at least forty centers operational, and at least ten other firms are entering the business. In these centers, a kind of performance contract to improve student achievement in certain areas is signed between the parents and the franchisee. The dollars that parents pay are over and above the property taxes they pay for the operation of the public schools. As these franchised centers expand, it is conceivable that parents in some areas will begin to withhold support from the public schools by defeating bond issues and even by insisting that taxes be reduced. In contrast, the process of educational engineering would allow the school system to utilize the services of various firms so as to renew themselves through the turnkey feature. Thus performance contracting can serve as a means for fostering structural reforms within a school system, thus allowing it to continue operations and become competitive with private schools and franchised learning centers without endangering the system.

Third, performance contracting allows a school system to experiment in an orderly, responsible manner with low costs and low political risks. Both school officials and critics have expressed the need to determine the relative cost effectiveness of various instructional methods, so that schools could estimate the costs both of initial adoption and of continued operation. In this sense, educational engineering allows board members to make rational, informed choices when choosing new techniques to be used in the regular curriculum.

Fourth, according to various court decisions, school systems are required to implement desegregation programs. Often the minority-group children have lower scores, sometimes drastically lower scores, on system-wide reading tests or other measures of educational achievement; and one of the worries of the favored community is that, upon integration, the presence of many students with low scores will hinder the progress of their own children. This worry can be considered quite apart from any issue of racism, not as an excuse for failing to integrate, but as a real problem that must be solved. Performance contracting can help us solve it. For example, we can easily set up a transitional program in which previously segregated children can gain their basic skills on a guaranteed basis while they are attending a newly integrated school. Thus, as we will discuss further in chapter eight, performance contracting can help communities to desegregate smoothly.

Finally, performance contracting, as part of a competitive process, can call forth a high quality both of proposals and of work. After all, the supplier's reputation (and, in the case of a private firm, his profits) depend on winning the contract and then meeting its specifications. Competition encourages diversity, thoroughness, and practicality. In this sense, educational engineering allows the school to concentrate on specifying what it wants to do and on running the programs it adopts. Between these two stages it calls on various outside agencies to help it in evolving, experimenting with, and assessing programs to meet its particular needs. In short, the performance contract is the flexible device through which the school calls in the necessary assistance and becomes, in fact, an open educational system.

Dwight W. Allen has said that "when educators look at technology as a resource for developing new alternatives and individualizing instruction, rather than as a dangerous, mechanistic intruder, then the existing wealth of technological developments will have its desired effect upon the world of education."[6] He introduced that statement, however, by suggesting that fear and ignorance now block the full use of technology. Perhaps we would all learn much more about the development of instructional technology if, instead of merely discussing it or toying with various models, we began actually to experiment with the wealth of developments through the medium of performance contracts, with the aid of management support groups, using development capital. This way, we can call on suppliers to match their promises, to adapt what is known to specific needs, and to deliver results.

6. Dwight W. Allen, Dean, School of Education, University of Massachusetts. Quote of page 37 of the *McMurrin Report*.

The
Independent
Educational
Accomplishment
Audit

Chapter 5

a S PREVIOUSLY DESCRIBED, the introduction of a third party to the student-school relationship can enhance formal education. Outside assessment of spending presently is required in science, business, government, and education.

No discovery or invention is accepted in science unless and until qualified third parties can verify the discovery or invention. Those who would establish something in science must describe conditions, results, and standards for others to reproduce. And every business, including the business of government and education, is subjected to a regular, recurring fiscal audit. Generally this review is done by certified public accountants using standards known to all. In the same way, providing an external review and assessing promised student accomplishment in terms of the conditions and standards of those who made the promises is essential to accountability in education.

Learning itself is a function of feedback — of knowledge of results. Without the evidence of an action or an activity, the learner cannot improve. Educational engineering leads us through a cycle, or, as an engineer might call it, a feedback loop. Once a school is provided with development capital and management support, and when the period of a performance contract comes to an end, the last stage of the cycle is the independent educational accomplishment audit. Through this arrangement we can gauge the results of a given program, as measured by what its students can do, and thus determine whether to continue the program and, if so, how to improve it.

The Drawbacks of Self-Assessment

Generally, the assessment of educational programs now suffers from three weaknesses. In most cases if it is done at all, it is done by the same people who ran the program rather than by outside auditors. Their report often gives less emphasis to student accomplishment than to the good intentions of planners and the complexity and inherent virtues of the program. And when actual results are tested, the assessment seldom takes full advantage of all the techniques available. To put it briefly and perhaps harshly, most current assessment is distorted, misdirected, and primitive.

In the short run, rosy self-assessments can aid a local school district or group of educational innovators in the competition for funds. Eventually, however, all such reports will be heavily discounted, and sharp critics will win a broad audience among parents, who, as voters, control the supply of public research funds. We have now reached this point of disillusionment. As educators, we should respond by pointing out that the current lack of funds for independent audits of educational results fails both as an economy measure and as a protection for professional egos. In the absence of impartial evaluation, we all suffer. How can we defend our stewardship of developmental funds? How can we even sort out the successful programs? How can we back up appeals for more funds?

Funding Educational Evaluation

In order to achieve an impartial, expert evaluation of results, we need funds earmarked for that purpose. So far the commitment to evaluation has been very slight. In fiscal 1969, for example, for every thousand dollars Congress provided for elementary and secondary programs, less than one dollar was used for evaluation of the results. As a result of this costly method for saving money, we literally do not know what good was done by the millions spent, nor do we know how to redirect our efforts. We do know from other indicators that education needs substantial federal aid; but as Congress responds to that need, it ought also to set aside an adequate portion of each appropriation for an audit of results.

In comparison to the inadequate attention still being paid to educational evaluation, the federal government spends $60 million on fiscal audits through the General Accounting Office alone, not to mention what is spent by individual agency audit teams. While educational evaluation and fiscal audits rely on somewhat different forms of analysis, in principle they are comparable; and as various federal agencies place increasing emphasis on evaluating the attainment of program goals as well as accounting for disbursed funds, the two forms of analysis tend to merge. Essentially, the new procedures match dollars spent against results achieved in order to show the cost effectiveness of a given program.

Congress and the Office of Education have begun to recognize the importance of these procedures, but the funds provided so far lag far behind the scope of evaluation requested. For example, of the slightly less than $250 million budget request for vocational education programs in fiscal 1969, only $490,000 was requested for all evaluation of the cost effectiveness of these programs, including the extent of employment of individuals completing them and the effectiveness of curriculum materials developed and distributed. To a local official, a lump sum of $490,000 may look like a lot of money, but when spread across 50 states and the localities within those states, the amounts available for evaluation of any given local program are severely inadequate.

An examination of management methods and operations in all phases of government is necessary from time to time. This helps assure that policies and procedures for getting maximum results from each tax dollar invested have been established. Naturally, education and its related functions make up a large and rapidly growing area of importance to the state and to individual taxpayers. Thus an evaluation of educational programs could be expected to yield valuable results in terms of an assessment of educational achievement and of the effective accomplishment of management objectives.

Fiscal Audits

At present, all levels of government are subject to a fiscal evaluation through an independent audit procedure. This is not only an accepted practice of good management, but a compulsory requirement. In education the fiscal audit is similarly required and, in many cases, must be advertised in the local newspaper and examined at a public hearing. On the federal level, too, when Congress appropriates huge sums of money for education, it requires fiscal auditing procedures for the disbursed funds.

Fiscal audits alone, however, fail to tell us whether the money was productively spent. It is not enough to know that officials are honest and reasonably careful. We also want some assessment of what results the money is producing. Fiscal audits account for the goods, facilities, and services paid for, but they tell us little about less tangible elements, such as the quality of management or the degree of educational accomplishment. If the same expense and effort now devoted to fiscal control were put into auditing our educational practices, we could swiftly weed out faulty procedures and programs that now persist thanks to dubious unchecked claims of success and, more important, we could spot the workable programs and nourish them accordingly.

National Assessment

This is not to say that studies and evaluation have not been conducted. Some long-range studies have been devoted to defining and assessing educational quality. For example, the U.S. Office of Education has invested a considerable amount of time and money in Project Talent, a sampling survey of several grade levels in various types of schools throughout the country; and it has directed studies of projects conducted under titles of the Elementary and Secondary Education Act, including studies of vocational education.

The shortcomings of these and similar assessments are that they are national in scope and provide scanty data on local projects; they are predominantly quantitative and reveal little of what actually occurs in the process of education; they are usually one-shot and fail to yield a continuing appraisal; and they are not coordinated with the assessment of other federal programs that often overlap and thus fail to show which program caused a given result. There remains a strong need for continued national studies, but such studies alone cannot be expected to provide information on whether federal dollars have effected change at the local level, what the nature of that change is, and most important, whether the change will endure.

Local Assessment

We recommend that along with the fiscal audit and the national assessment procedures, the federal government stimulate coordinated educational accomplishment audits at the local level. Furthermore, we believe that when Congress enacted education laws, it did intend such educational audits as a necessary complement to other control procedures. For example, in Public Law 89-10, written in 1964, Congress repeatedly referred to the assessment of educational results, providing for "appropriate objective measurements of educational achievement . . . for evaluating at least annually the effectiveness of the program . . ." and for procedures to show "the extent to which funds . . . have been effective in improving educational opportunities of persons in the area served. . . ."[1]

In order to achieve accountability in education, provisions such as these must be defined much more sharply, supported with adequate funds for assessment, applied more broadly, and above all enforced. Although accountability might apply in theory to many aspects of education we would limit its application here to the acquisition of basic skills, or to the aspect of education commonly called training. Similarly, although all students undergo training in basic skills, we are especially accountable to those now failed by their schools, such as the "disadvantaged" child who does not learn to read. Where the school system seems to be working, nobody worries about accountability, though perhaps they should; but where new and heavy demands cause the system obviously to falter, parents and students as well as those who appropriate funds are entitled to hold the schools accountable for revising their program to ensure results.

The independent educational accomplishment audit is the device through which the public can hold its school accountable, and also through which the school can learn how to improve its programs in order to meet the demands rightly made by its constituency. Concern among the electorate for results in education is a relatively recent development. It is apparent that we have moved from the stage of providing resources for student opportunities to a demand for information about the extent to which the resources have resulted in student learning. This is especially true of the educational benefits called basic skills. This shift can be seen in the brief history of the Elementary and Secondary Education Act of 1965. This act concentrated massive federal resources on the problems of institutional renewal and direct service to the poor and disadvantaged. It provided equipment, teachers, space, books, and the like. In the years since the act was passed, however, questions put by congressional committees have moved far beyond how the money was spent and for whom, to whether the students are learning and securing jobs or falling behind. This insistence on accountability for results is the political soil in which the new independent accomplishment audit is growing.

---

1. Section 205(a) (5) and Title III, respectively.

The Independent Accomplishment Audit

Each word in this phrase was chosen to express an aspect of the procedure, and a closer look at each of these elements may help us to explain the concept of an independent accomplishment audit.

First, *independent.* The community served by a school usually has little choice in the information and reports given it by the teachers, administrators, and boards of education. Citizens and students generally are in no position to ask that information be prepared according to their specifications, nor, except for the mandated fiscal reports, do they have assurance that information given out is adequate, or prepared according to some set of ground rules.

Bureaucracies in the field of education, as in other fields, tend to withhold information from the public except when required to provide it or when struggles within the bureaucracy produce a news leak. Under these conditions, even when data does reach the public, the information is often out of context or is otherwise mis-leading, irrelevant to the concerns felt by the public, and unreli-able anyway. To the extent that a bureaucracy treats everyone out-side it as an intruder, even in the case of those who support it with their taxes and who are supposed to be served by it, the public obviously needs its own source of information about the workings of that bureaucracy, a source that is impartial, reliable, informa-tive, and regular. Inevitably, this calls for an outside agency charged by the public with the duty to audit the affairs of the bureaucracy and to report its findings openly.

A distinctive feature of the independent accomplishment audit is the concept of a third-party review to assess the "truth" as seen by outside reviewers free of local ties and interests. This offers protection not only to the public, but also to the bureaucracy under review, which might otherwise suffer unfair attacks. When a third party examines educational results, the local parties can have con-fidence in the impartiality of the findings, and if the auditor is trained and experienced in the field, they can use his findings as the basis for deciding on next steps, instead of feuding over what the facts might be or, even worse, arguing in terms of theories apart from any reference to the local situation. Outside review is of fundamental importance in both business and government; its use in the area of instruction can help both the educators and their constituencies to be responsible and effective.

In outlining the features of an independent accomplishment audit, let us next consider the word *accomplishment*. Every organization has, or at least is intended to have, outputs. Even though we may not always be able readily to measure or even to define these outputs, we recognize that every organization does, or tries to do, something. In education what the organization does is to provide teachers and other personnel, materials, space, and certain processes such as what apparently occurs in a given classroom, or at least what is said and visibly done there. From the viewpoint of an educator, the output of the school is thus often defined in terms of services provided. For example, an educator could tell us that his school provides tenth graders with so many hours of geometry, using a certain approach to the subject and corresponding materials, taught by a man with a specified number of credits, in a class of so many students, meeting in a room that meets minimum standards of size, lighting, heat, and so forth. Less precisely, he could go on to discuss the level of teacher morale, the beauty of the architectural surrounding, or the background, preparation, and attitude of the students; and he might mention other factors as well. From the viewpoint of a student, the output of the school might look quite different. One student might feel that geometry is irrelevant, the teacher confusing and authoritarian. Another might find his class endlessly absorbing as he sets out to prove the impossibility of trisecting an angle using only a compass and a straightedge.

In making an accomplishment audit, however, we focus neither on the services apparently provided by the school nor on the process of attending school as experienced by the students, but rather on what the students are able to do as a result of taking part in a given program. In other words, we look at educational results, not at the everyday life of the school, whether seen by an educator or by a student. For years we have looked primarily at what the educators proposed to do and what they said they were doing, in the form of curriculum guides, progress reports, and various program descriptions. As in the case of accomplishment auditing, so in the case of process reporting: we need searching, extended reports by independent observers, and these reports ought to focus no less on the views of students than on the plans and self-evaluations of educators. Skillful reports on the actual process of education, from a variety of viewpoints, can help us understand some of the reasons behind educational accomplishment or its lack. This, however, is not the purpose of the independent accomplishment audit itself. When the auditors go to a school they set aside their interests in the process of teaching in favor of measuring student learning. They go less to inquire what the schools do than to assess how much the students have learned.

A word about measurement is essential. Measurement is applied judgment. Judgments can be made on the basis of interviews, observations, and instruments, such as tests or videotapes. Society at large makes use of a variety of modes of proof as measures for action. Thus Congress uses the hearing as a means of guiding its decisions for the allocation of billions of dollars. We use juries to "measure" a man's innocence or guilt. We "prove" our reliability through taking an oath or going to a notary. The expert witness is frequently called on to render a measurement in the form of a judgment. People sign petitions indicating their judgment or measure of something. These modes of proof can be, have been, and should be a vital part of education. They become practical in the hands of skilled people called accomplishment auditors.

Through the use of small-sample statistical techniques, thorough judgments of small numbers of students can indicate the performance of the entire student population under review. What do the students know? What can they do? This is what the auditors judge. The techniques they use may range from forms as loose and revealing as interviews to forms as narrow and exact as multiple-choice tests. Are the auditors competent, unbiased, and thorough? Does their judgment go to the questions in which the community, including parents, is interested? In other words, do the auditors report reliably on relevant accomplishment? We ought to have auditors professional enough to do so.

Finally, let us discuss the word *audit*. In general an audit is a standard review conducted, as we have said, by someone who is qualified and trusted to make objective reports. During the early years of public education in America, first, school board members, and later, superintendents and other officials inspected the schools. Rudiments of this inspection process persist in many school systems' annual testing programs and occasional visits by school officials. The independent accomplishment audit, however, exists not as a reincarnation of the old inspection process but rather as a new kind of management feedback loop — a management-by-reflection process, as we might call it.

Management by reflection may be an apt phrase for the regularized use of independent accomplishment audits. We can see it in its simplest form in local school use of federal discretionary money. Local people write a proposal for funds awarded on a competitive basis, that is, given to the "best" proposals. In the proposal, they make certain promises about what they will accomplish with the funds. They stipulate what students will be able to do as a result of the program, under what conditions learning will take place, and what standards will be sought or applied in judging it. Independent accomplishment auditing, or management by reflection, takes students, replicates the conditions detailed in the proposal, notes the performance of the students, applies the standards, and thereby makes a public report of the promises delivered.

The Effects of the IAA

Consider how the provision for an outside assessment of results can affect a school system. When a program is being planned, the auditors are called in to help clarify the objectives in measurable terms. When the program begins, they test the participants, as they do again when the program is completed. Then they report the results. In this partnership between local school officials and the independent auditors, the objectives are set within the system, and the accomplishment is assessed from outside. The partnership offers several advantages. It induces a problem-solving mode of thought in which general goals are augmented by carefully defined, measurable objectives. Since auditing sorts out the programs that work, it helps good educational practice become standard practice as soon as the evidence is acted on. And since the judgment of an experienced impartial outsider always carries more weight than the reassurances of the official whose program is under review, the audit can reverse the drift toward suspicion of and disenchantment with some of our schools, a feeling already reflected in school bond defeats and reductions in federal aid to education. The electorate will surely be less reluctant to pay for programs that can bear the light of thorough outside scrutiny and of public reports of the findings.

The IAA's Six Basic Stages

The independent accomplishment audit has six essential stages: the pre-audit, the translation of local goals into demonstrable data, the adoption or development of instrumentation and methodology, the establishment of a review calendar, the assessment process, and the public report. Let us briefly consider each of these stages.

In the *pre-audit*, the objectives of the particular program are discussed by the auditor selected and by representatives of those who have an interest in the program, namely its planners, its intended beneficiaries, its staff, and the community that supports it. Together they produce and agree on a list of local objectives and a clear description of the programs in some order of priority. In the case of performance contracts, the auditor reviews the procedures manual supplied by the agency that gives the money.

In the *translation* stage, the auditor and his local clients determine what evidence will indicate whether the objectives have been met and how it will be gathered. In other words, they specify what the students should be able to do as a result of the educational experience, the conditions that promote that performance, and the standards to be applied in interpreting the program's success.

This discussion naturally leads to the *instrumentation* stage, in which the auditor, still working with the local education authority, chooses the auditing instruments, such as specific tests, questionnaires, interview protocols, and unobtrusive measures, specified by local leadership, that will be used to collect the data. The product of this stage is a specific list of defined techniques and procedures.

Next, the parties agree on a *review calendar*. This written document indicates the nature of the assessments, where they will be held, how long they will take, when they will occur, who will be responsible for arrangements, and other logistical considerations. In a sense, this document becomes part of the contract between the auditor and the local education authority. It assures that the terms of the audit are set in advance and will not be adjusted later to disguise shortcomings in the program or to focus exclusively on a partial success.

Once these four stages are completed, the educational program begins. At its conclusion the auditor returns to conduct the *assessment process* itself. In this stage, the team of auditors carries out the procedures agreed on earlier and specified in the review calendar. Albert V. Mayerhofer of the U.S. Office of Education suggests that, depending on the complexity of the program being reviewed, an accomplishment audit need take only ten school days per year for a given school district (and much less time, of course, for any given class). His idea is to send completely equipped and staffed mobile vans from city to city each year so that overhead costs of salaries and equipment can be shared. Many other organizational forms are possible.

Finally, the auditor files a *public report* at an open meeting, in which he indicates in specific terms both the accomplishments of the program and ways in which it might be improved. With this information, and with comparative data on the cost effectiveness of other types of programs conducted elsewhere, the school board can reach relatively informed decisions on which programs deserve further support.

Terms such as cost effectiveness may arouse fears that criteria will be narrowly or mechanistically defined in a style more applicable to deciding what aircraft to buy than to fashioning a curriculum. This need not be so. No system of assessment is better than its criteria, but in education, as in other fields that serve human needs, we can frame our criteria and *then* find the necessary measures, rather than constricting our goals to match primitive assessment techniques. In the pre-audit stage, the discussion begins not with a consideration of what the auditor can most easily measure, but with an exploration of what the school officials hope to accomplish; and as these goals are translated into performance criteria, the auditor may find that he must adapt existing tests or develop new ones, and that he must add new techniques of assessment. In this partnership between school and auditor, the goals of the school will stimulate new means of assessment no less than the use of the independent accomplishment audit will encourage the broad adoption of programs that work.

The Importance of Specific Performance Criteria
The key to this process is the framing of objectives in terms of performance. Let us see why. If I live in Detroit and have as my objective a visit by road to Los Angeles, it is not sufficient merely to be told that the direction is southwest. I need more specific instructions. Similarly in education, the general direction of faculty to teach students "to understand and appreciate science" is insufficient. To be useful, the general direction must be supplemented with a set of operational steps. Thus we might supplement the science objective mentioned above by listing such projects as

the dissection of a frog in a science laboratory, or we might ask the student to demonstrate an application of Ohm's Law in an experiment with electricity. The ability to perform a set of these projects would not guarantee that a student understood or appreciated science, but at least he would be much nearer that goal than a student who was baffled by projects such as these.

General objectives, goals, or purposes serve a useful purpose, but American education suffers no shortage of them. On the other hand, we do need more performance criteria that clearly specify the student competency to be displayed, the methods for displaying it, and the standards for judging whether it is sufficient. For example, we can specify that 90 percent of all students should score 90 percent or higher on a given test of reading based on certain materials. Auditors and local officials will discuss, in advance, which tests to use and what numbers are acceptable, but the performance criteria, however they are phrased, must always be specific.

In some cases a school may wish to specify a complex audit involving a variety of measures. In addition to standardized tests that are relatively simple to administer, the school might call for observations of lab or field performance, videotapes of certain procedures, interviews, discussions, and classroom observations. Along with widespread testing, the auditors can draw a random sample of the student population and use the methods just mentioned to explore the learning of the small sample much more thoroughly than they could with the group as a whole.

The whole basis of science is independent verification. If I claim to have developed a serum to cure cancer, I must have my discovery independently verified by a jury of professional experts. The point is not that they necessarily suspect my work. No matter how plausible the hypothesis or eminent the discoverer, no scientific result is acceptable until someone else, using appropriate procedures, obtains the same results. Thus every scientific accomplishment is, in effect, independently audited within a profession that knows how to specify conditions and set standards. In this sense, the independent accomplishment audit proposed for our schools has precedents not only in fiscal auditing but also in the scientific practice of independent verification.

Training the Educational Auditor
In order to live up to these analogies, the educational auditor needs

the training and support enjoyed by other professionals. Where is it to be found? Presently the eighty-six projects under the bilingual and dropout prevention programs (Titles VII and VIII of the Elementary and Secondary School Act) are being reviewed by independent accomplishment auditors. These early experimental audits are being conducted by groups including private firms such as Booz, Allen, and Hamilton and Dunlop Associates, and nonprofit organizations such as Educational Testing Service and Evaluative Programs for Innovative Curriculums (EPIC), a regional testing laboratory supported by the federal government.

Several major universities are preparing courses in educational auditing; examples include Georgia State University, Florida State, and the University of California at Riverside. In May 1970 the Bureau of Education Personnel Development of the U.S. Office of Education began to let RFPs to stimulate the training of educational auditors. There is a large body of knowledge about assessment in the military and industrial sectors as well as in such fields as sociology, anthropology, and psychological measurement. It is possible to contemplate the growth of a new professional career, that of certified educational auditor. Standards for such certification could be established by state departments of education or by a private society.[2]

Since a growing number of federal programs in education will probably require auditing, the U.S. Office of Education might take a strong role in designing audit systems, training local personnel in audit procedures, developing management systems for cost-effective administration, arranging a network of independent resource personnel to consult regularly with local school systems, and accumulating and disseminating data on successful reforms in education.

The new auditing professionals will at first be drawn from those trained in systems analysis, psychological measurement, and social statistics. As the movement spreads, extensive training will have to be done to meet the demand. Some of this training will occur in universities, some in centers supported by the government, some within private firms, some in non-profit organizations. In these various places of training, systems analysts will have to learn more about the special problems of education, and those who

2. The author is now helping to found a national society of educational engineers, one of whose major functions might be to set performance standards for auditors.

come from the field of education will learn more about the use of sophisticated measurements as part of a management feedback loop.

In fact, the application of this feedback loop to educational reform will assure that auditors become more than a new corps of test administrators and record keepers. The sources of their dignity and usefulness are several. First, they will work as professionals. They will not only be qualified for certification, but also will be employed by a group independent of the organization they audit. Second, they will report not only to their immediate client, the school, but to the broader constituency the school exists to serve. Thus reports will not merely be filed but will be accessible to the whole community to serve as a basis for planning and reform. Third, the auditing profession will not only administer instruments and procedures already available, but will constantly develop new methods to meet their clients' needs. Fourth, when schools use a performance contract (as explained in the preceding chapter), the results shown by the independent audit will mean dollars won or lost by the private firm that holds the contract, a situation that will encourage swift adoption of lessons learned. In summary, the accomplishment auditor is independent, responsible to the public, and equipped both to innovate within his own profession and to encourage reforms within the schools.

The Process at Work: Texarkana

Chapter 6

HOW DO ALL THE ELEMENTS of educational engineering come together in actual practice? So far we have outlined the concept of accountability and the process designed to provide it, including such elements as development capital, management support, outside instructional services, and the independent accomplishment audit. Each of them offers a new form of assistance to the schools and together they can help us engineer a working instructional technology. This process, however, is no longer simply an idea: its practice in the public schools began in December 1968.

In that month, a talented and persuasive young consultant sold the idea of educational engineering to the schools of Texarkana, a community straddling the border of Arkansas and Texas. This chapter will describe the resulting project, not in terms of its educational results (which are yet to be officially audited), but rather as an early example of the process recommended by this book. In itself, the Texarkana dropout prevention program is no more than one project, run by one firm, in one small city. High achievement there would not necessarily guarantee a similar result elsewhere, nor would a modest outcome mean that educational engineering has little to offer.[1] Judgment of the process must wait until we have a variety of experience: meanwhile, what educational engineering needs is not ballyhoo but opportunities to show what it can do in many different settings.

It is worth repeating that, unlike many plans for the reform of the schools, educational engineering is neither a set of principles

1. It is important to keep in mind that educational engineering is not a program of instruction but a way of developing a variety of programs for many purposes. Thus its value rests not on the outcome of any single program but rather on the aggregate value of a whole range of programs run by many different firms in a variety of settings. We also face problems in measuring results reliably. Teachers may "teach the test," especially when they want their students to do well on an outside test. When profits depend on scores in such tests, as they do in performance contracting, we need to insulate the instructional program from the process of testing. This is one reason the accomplishment auditors should be independent of both the school and the firm.

nor a particular instructional program. Instead, it is a flexible process through which schools can enlist a coordinated group of outside resources that can help to pay for, define, provide, and evaluate programs to meet local goals. Just as mechanical engineering can be turned to many different jobs, so this process goes beyond any single philosophy of education (except a belief in effectiveness), any particular machinery or method of instruction, and any one educational objective. Above all, the process offers flexibility and responsiveness: instead of starting with all manner of outside ideas and then dumping the final program on an overburdened school, educational engineering begins with the particular needs of the school and then calls on various forms of substantive outside help in order to meet them.

The Texarkana Approach

Texarkana had one set of needs in the area of dropout prevention, and its project embodies one set of responses. Its approach to the problem, however, shows us the broad outlines of educational engineering. Other projects will develop in their own ways, according to the specifications set, the local conditions, and the help available, but we can adapt the approach pioneered in Texarkana to the problems of many kinds of schools in teaching the basic skills. In this chapter, therefore, we place more emphasis on the transportable process than on the welter of details in Texarkana itself.[2]

In 1968 when the story begins, Texarkana faced a severe dropout problem, soon to be aggravated by pressures to integrate the schools. In the part of town lying in Arkansas, for example, students at a predominantly white, middle-class junior high school ranked in the seventy-fifth percentile on the Iowa Tests of Basic Skills. At another junior high, however, where the races were about equally mixed and the average family income was somewhat lower, student achievement averaged in the twentieth percentile, and at a junior high in an all-black neighborhood, the average was no higher than the second percentile.

Apart from any racial issue, school officials thus faced the question of how to integrate children who were well above average in

2. So far the most comprehensive early account known to the author is "Texarkana: The First Accounting," a thoughtful story by Richard A. Bumstead, Features Editor of *Educate* magazine, published in its March 1970 issue, pages 24-37.

reading with others who could barely read a line. Would the drop-out rate, already worrisome, rise sharply as formerly segregated children had to face competition from far more accomplished peers? Would parents of children who had been taught how to read have educational grounds for opposing integration? If so, what would happen to the community, faced with a cutoff of federal funds? Could a way be found to avoid both disruption and delay, to remove reading deficiencies in some kind of accelerated program? Where could the money be found, and who could possibly produce the educational results the schools so urgently needed?

Charles Blaschke, an educational consultant based in Washington, was alerted to the situation in Texarkana by a friend who was working there in the Model Cities program. With training in economics and public administration, Blaschke had already worked as acting chief of educational technology for the Office of Economic Opportunity and, during his military service, in the office of the Secretary of Defense during McNamara's last years. While there, he ran a study of how effectively the armed forces had been using new instructional technology in their training programs. Upon leaving the Pentagon he joined a management consulting firm, seeking an opportunity to apply what he had learned to problems faced by the public schools in teaching basic skills.

Going to Texarkana on his own initiative, Blaschke proposed to school officials there that instead of trying to solve their problem unassisted, they specify the educational accomplishment they wanted to produce; let him write a proposal for federal funds under the dropout prevention program; send out a request for proposals and invite firms in the education business to submit their bids. The idea was that a firm could use its own methods without disrupting the rest of the school, and could be held to the strict performance criteria stated in the contract. Blaschke pointed out that if the program should fail, the contractor would bear the burden, and if it worked, as he expected it would, the schools could thus help many children who, in effect, had reluctantly been given up for lost. He added that if the firm were required to train local personnel in the operation of the program, the schools could easily absorb it into their regular curriculum when the contract expired; and that if the federal grant would pay for preliminary planning and management support, the whole project would require a bare minimum of extra work by the school system itself.

How could they lose? The Texarkana school districts told Blaschke to go ahead and write the proposal. Only ten months later the program began. What happened between December 1969, when local school officials decided to see what might come of the newfangled idea of educational engineering, and October 1969, when a firm called Dorsett opened its facilities in or near several of the Texarkana schools?

The Texarkana Proposal

On December 18, 1969, the U.S. Office of Education received the preliminary proposal for a dropout prevention program; and on March 10, 1969, with the support of the author (who was then Associate U.S. Commissioner of Education), it granted Texarkana $20,000 for preparation of a detailed, formal proposal.[3] Working with Blaschke and with representatives of teachers, students, and the community, school officials hammered out their proposal and submitted it on May 3rd to the Office of Education which, on May 19th, announced a grant of $250,000 for the first phase of the program in Texarkana. On June 10th school officials, with the help of their management support group, sent a document called "request for proposal" to 113 potential bidders in the education industry. As the first of its kind, this fourteen-page document is worth a close look.[4]

In its request for proposal (RFP), Texarkana first set a few general conditions. No contractor would be considered unless (1) the firm was willing to be reimbursed "on the basis of student achievement per maximum periods of instructional time, with heavy penalties for failure to meet performance standards"; (2) its instructional process was "relatively non-labor intensive" and also "individualized and self-pacing to the greatest extent possible"; and

3. This whole approach was made possible by the Dropout Prevention Amendment that Senator George Murphy sponsored in 1968. Under this amendment, the Bureau of Elementary and Secondary Education developed guidelines providing for the submission of brief, standardized preliminary proposals that would clearly define the educational deficit for which aid was being sought and for an equal competition for program money through the award of planning grants to local districts. With the planning grant, a local district could retain a management support group to help in drafting the formal proposal. The amendment also encouraged the concentration of available funds on a workable number of carefully designed programs, rather than spreading the money far and wide, and provided funds for hiring an independent educational accomplishment auditor.

4. Portions of it appeared in *Educational Technology*, August 1969, pages 5-9; and it is presented as an exhibit at the back of this book.

(3) the program, once demonstrated, could be "implemented into the counterpart grade levels within the local system without creating unnecessary political and social problems within the community." In other words, the firm had to propose a program that was relatively inexpensive; that relied on some of the new technology rather than on more teachers; that could later be taken over easily by the school itself; and that meanwhile would assure the necessary educational results, in the case of students who were in danger of leaving school.

Response to the RFP

Who would dare to accept such a challenge? No fewer than forty private firms sent representatives to Texarkana for a pre-bidding conference in late June 1969; and by mid-August ten of them had submitted full proposals.[5] Consider the odds against this response: apart from the novelty of the arrangement and sheer difficulty of the task, firms had to face the uncertainty of federal funding for the project; the risk of widespread publicity in case of failure to meet the performance criteria; questions about the practicality of these criteria; the distant location and the social problems of Texarkana; and doubts about how much freedom the winning bidder would have to run his program without interference.[6]

Consider, too, what a firm was being asked to do. According to the request for proposal, the typical student in the dropout prevention program, although not below average in intelligence, would come from a low-income, poorly-educated family, have low motivation, and be two or three grade levels behind his ninth grade peers in math, in reading, or both, and would be similarly deficient in study skills. In working with these students, the schools clearly

5. The firms which bid for the contract were: Behavioral Research Laboratories, Washington, D.C. and Palo Alto, California; Dorsett Educational Systems, Norman, Oklahoma; Edcon, Inc., Alexandria, Virginia; Educational Development Laboratory, Inc., (a division of McGraw-Hill), Huntington, New York; Interactive Learning Systems, Inc., Boston, Massachusetts; Learning Foundations, Inc., Athens, Georgia; Macmillan Educational Services, Beverly Hills, California; Plan Education Centers, Inc., Little Rock, Arkansas; Quality Educational Development, Inc., Washington, D.C.; and RCA Service Co., Camden, New Jersey. In the exhibits section of this book we give an excerpt from the proposal made by Dorsett, the firm that won the Texarkana contract. This excerpt represents only one of hundreds of approaches possible within performance contracting.

6. In this paragraph and in the following general discussion of the proposals, the author is relying in part on an unpublished report prepared by Laurence L. Belanger for the U.S. Office of Education and extensive discussions with him.

had fallen behind. What could an outside firm possibly do to help them? What approach would it take?

Proposals varied widely. All of them stressed the need for students to be actively involved, not seated passively as in regular classrooms; and toward this end the proposals emphasized individually paced instruction and a variety of motivational measures, including a day-by-day report to each student on his progress. All the firms proposed using the new instructional technology. Some emphasized technology in the sense of hardware; others placed more confidence in relationships between teachers and students. Some included plans for extrinsic rewards in the form of tokens or trading stamps; others depended more on intrinsic kinds of reward. Some proposed to use instructional programs already developed elsewhere; others offered to prepare custom-made materials and media to fit the situation. Some appeared willing to employ incumbent school personnel in a variety of resourceful ways; others were somewhat less dependent on local resources.

No proposal suggested an entirely new approach, nor was it expected that they would. In general, the resources are available and can be supplied "off the shelf." In addition to their relative familiarity with these items, the firms offered a much more imaginative mix of resources than is usually found in our schools. For example, one corporation proposed to combine three instructional management systems and convert existing Job Corps materials to a new media format. Another firm was prepared to install an audio-visual learning system that had been under development for twelve years, and to combine it with various software published by other corporations. A third company wanted to employ a computer-based counseling system that had been used elsewhere but would have been new to the Southwest.

On the whole the proposals showed considerable ingenuity and reflected the best thought in this particular field. Confronted with the Texarkana request for proposal, these firms were able, in a very short time, to combine ideas, technology, staff, and cost proposals to meet local needs. Thus, when the school officials of Texarkana sat down in August 1969, they no longer had to consider the dropout program merely in terms of local resources, as before;[7]

7. Consultants named by the firms included such distinguished scholars and educators as Drs. Robert Branson, Caleb Cattengo, Jim Evans, Lloyd Homme, Robert Mager, John McKee, Robert Morgan, and Glen Valentine.

instead, they were able to discuss detailed proposals from ten firms that had experience in the field, access to top consultants, and familiarity with the latest technology.

Reactions to the Texarkana Project

In August 1969, about when firms were submitting their bids to Texarkana, several interesting stories and comments on the project appeared. In *Educational Technology* that month, the editor observed that the Texarkana project was "unique in several respects: (1) This is the first time a public school has contracted with a private firm to provide academic instruction for its students. (2) This is the first use of performance contracting within a public school system. (3) This is the first time a school system has utilized the services of a management support group. (4) This is the first attempt by a school system to utilize a separately managed and operated center in order to determine the cost effectiveness of new educational technology approaches and, based on this credible demonstration, to integrate proven techniques into the schools' curricula."[8]

The *Wall Street Journal* reported that "private industry is beginning to bid for a significant new plan in public education—far beyond anything so humdrum as supplying textbooks, films or records"; that success in Texarkana "could give the winner a convincing competitive advantage in merchandising its teaching wares elsewhere and could provide the new technology with its first major entry into the public school market"; that the contractor "must promise to bring backward Texarkana students up to normal grades for their age levels at a given cost and in a given time—or else pay a money penalty"; and that "the basic goal is to gain specific educational results rather than simply hire more teachers, purchase more books, or furnish more special services. . . ."[9]

In placing this article in the *Congressional Record*, the Chairman of the House Subcommittee on General Education, Rep. Roman C. Pucinski, hailed the Texarkana program as "a concept

8. "Performance Contracting as Catalyst for Reform," *Educational Technology*, August 1969, editor's note, page 5.

9. Jonathan Spivak, "Firms Vie to Show How to Halt Dropouts in Arkansas Schools," *Wall Street Journal*, August 12, 1969. The story also noted that "up to now, many federal education programs have concentrated on such means rather than the ends to be attained. . . ."

in American education which in my judgment offers great promise of major breakthroughs in raising achievement skills for our nation's young people"; promised to "watch this experiment closely for, indeed, if it succeeds in Texarkana it is a concept that we will want to employ throughout the country"; observed that "private industry has much to offer in educational technology"; and hoped that the pattern pioneered in Texarkana would "give overworked teachers in this country the assistance they can get from these major breakthroughs . . ."[10]

About a week later the *Dallas Morning News* ran a commentary on the Texarkana project, describing it as "an encouraging attempt by government to break out of the dreary pattern of failure by concentrating on the job of deciding and then assigning the doing to those who can meet performance standards." The writer declared that unlike a government bureaucracy, which "tends to perpetuate its failures," private organizations, especially those which must earn a profit, tend to "abandon an experiment that fails and try another approach—remember the Edsel?" The writer further declared that government ought to delegate more of the work that needs doing, once it has decided "which problems require the most immediate effort and how much . . . what it wants done about them, what results it can reasonably expect to achieve." He noted that in Texarkana, "the government is not going to try to do the job itself, but will contract the educational task out to private industry" and "will set performance requirements and hold the contractor responsible for achieving the required results . . ."[11]

Evaluating the Proposals

As interest in the new approach began to mount, officials in Texarkana began to study the various proposals with the help of their management support group. Each firm had an opportunity to make a formal presentation to the local school officials and to answer their questions. With the experience of preparing the request for proposal and of reviewing the bids, the school officials were fully prepared to talk business language and, when the occasion war-

10. Hon. Roman C. Pucinski, "The Coming Revolution in American Education," *Congressional Record*, August 13, 1969, page E7021.

11. Jim Wright, "Feds Decide, Then Delegate the Doing," *Dallas Morning News*, August 21, 1969.

ranted, to use it against the firms. At one point in his presentation, a representative claimed that his proposal for heavy reliance on teaching machines was cost effective simply because it was relatively inexpensive. He was interrupted by a board member who pointed out that although cost effectiveness is a ratio between costs and results, the representative had spoken only of the former, not at all of the educational accomplishment his firm would be able to guarantee.

Even when all the figures were in, the bids were difficult to compare. Officials of course expected that in content, philosophy, and process, the various instructional programs would differ, but it turned out that the cost breakdowns were surprisingly complex. Because of delays in this evaluative phase, a letter of intent in place of a final contract between the contractor and the school districts was necessary in order to get the project started on time. The contract itself, the first of its kind, called for careful negotiation and review, not only by Texarkana and Dorsett Educational Systems, the winning bidder, but also by the U.S. Office of Education, which was supporting the whole project. Nonetheless, in early September, less than a month after bids were due, the letter of intent was signed; and in mid-October the first "rapid learning center" was opened by Dorsett in Texarkana. Meanwhile the Office of Education suggested that the parties drop provisions for a contractor performance bond, work-study training, and the testing of students for retention, but add more rigorous penalty features and an upper limit on total payments that the contractor could earn. On December 1, 1969, the final contract was approved.[12]

The Texarkana Contract

In general terms, this contract provided that the contractor would instruct a minimum of 200 students in basic reading, math, and study skills until June 5, 1970; that the students would be drawn equally from volunteers, students assigned by counselors, and students randomly selected from those with a grade-level deficiency of 2.0 or more; that instruction would occur in several rapid learning centers located in schoolrooms and in a mobile facility; that the program would use teaching machines manufactured by the

12. Major excerpts from the contract appear in the exhibits section of this book.

contractor; that, along with its other staff, the contractor would employ part-time at least twenty Texarkana teachers and administrators in order to "facilitate the contemplated transfer" of the program to the schools when the contract expired; and that Texarkana would pay the contractor $80 for each student who increased one grade level in reading or math within eighty hours of instruction "or proportionally for each fraction thereof." If the contractor raised a child one grade level in less time, he would be paid more, up to a limit of roughly $106 for doing the job in sixty hours or less; and if he took longer than 110 hours, the amount paid would steadily fall so that no payment at all would be made if the job took 168 hours or more.[13]

Its Precedent-setting Features

What is most important about this contract is not the particular method or scale of payment agreed on, but three features that set precedents in the field of education: (1) once the school officials had specified the results they wanted, the contractor was free to propose his own methods for achieving those results and, in this case, to operate in rapid learning centers outside of the regular school program; (2) compensation for the services provided was linked directly to the educational results actually produced, as determined by an independent auditor; and (3) the methods and staffing of the program were designed so that, if results were as good as expected, the contractor could simply turn the keys over to the local schools and the program can go on without disruption.

Problem Areas

These features can help us open a new era of instructional technology, but we must do more than incant them as a magic formula for curing all our ills. Any process, no matter how promising, calls for a lot of work, self-criticism, adaptability, and resourcefulness. In various areas of educational engineering, our skills are primitive. Some of these areas will be discussed further in chapter eight, but meanwhile let us consider the problem of testing.

---

13. In the request for proposal, potential bidders were also offered an all or nothing payment scheme, according to which the school would pay an agreed amount when a student demonstrated the minimum necessary increase in accomplishment, and nothing at all if the increase were not shown within an agreed number of hours in instruction.

In order to explore the full potential of performance contracting, we obviously need more reliable and broad-ranging methods of measuring educational accomplishment. In Texarkana, negotiations between school officials and the contractor were bedeviled by the imprecision of the testing instruments. In a searching article on the program, the project manager for Dorsett is quoted as saying:

> Suppose three students walk into an RLC (rapid learning center) with a paper saying they are at the 6.2 grade level. One could be a non-reader who happened to be lucky on the test. Give a kid an answer sheet but no test and he can turn in a score of 6.2 in reading ability. . . . The second student could be performing at exactly the 6.2 level. The third could be reading at the tenth grade level but didn't feel like taking a test that day.[14]

In these circumstances, how can a firm afford to agree to use a nationally normed reference test to measure individual student achievement, especially when its profits depend on the results? Experts working in Texarkana believe that future programs should use criterion-referenced tests. Undoubtedly we can improve testing procedures in many other ways as well, but this example is enough to remind us of the problems.

Another problem area is the turnkey provision through which schools are able to adopt successful programs easily into their own regular curriculum. Will they do so? Ultimately, educational engineering is intended to renew the school itself, not only to create supplementary or compensatory programs outside of it. The very reason these programs are needed is that many schools are failing at part of their job. If educational engineering could merely rescue the potential dropouts, as in Texarkana, it would be doing a considerable service. But why stop there? Why wait until a student has wasted years in school and been taught to regard himself as a failure — why wait until then to apply modern methods? In short, why not integrate those methods into the curriculum so that he learns the basic skills on his first time around? We can do so if we work out the details of the turnkey feature: so far, of course, nobody has got to this point, except in making proposals. Like the vagaries of testing, this is another problem in educational engineering that we must face.

---

14. Article by Richard A. Bumstead, cited above in footnote 2.

Implications of the Texarkana Program

Apart from the problems found in any process, however, we can also mention some early examples of success, in Texarkana and in our profession as a whole. In its first trial, educational engineering has shown that outside management support can help produce effects that local officials had not dared to imagine were possible, given the constraints as viewed from within a system. It has shown that the education industry will bid energetically for a performance contract and, drawing on the latest technology, put together programs, otherwise unavailable, that are responsive to local needs. It has shown, too, in the words of an editorial note *in Nation's Schools*, that ". . . if funds for education depend on educational output, not input, then schools will be concerned with learning, not teaching, and the development of a science of performance measurement may create a new type of educational planning in this country."[15]

Finally, we might recall that when Texarkana decided to try performance contracting, the city was disturbed about the effects of impending desegregation of the schools. There, as elsewhere in the United States, one of the major fears of the white community is that educationally deficient black children will hold back white children, thus lowering the overall quality of instruction in the newly integrated schools. In Texarkana, this fear was allayed because the contractor guaranteed to bring these children up to a level such that, upon full-time integration into the regular program of the schools, after part-time work in the rapid learning centers, black children would be able to share the school work of their white peers, even though they had started, on the average, some seventy percentiles behind them at the ninth-grade level.

Texarkana is the hometown of the national Freedom of Choice Movement, which is designed to offset desegregation attempts. By the time that the U.S. Office of Education announced in May 1969, that the school districts in Texarkana would receive nearly $250,000 to conduct the new dropout prevention program, one of the districts had submitted a freedom of choice plan that had been turned down by the Department of Health, Education and Welfare. When the school board of this district found that it would not be allowed to participate in the new program because of non-compliance

15. *Nation's Schools*, December, 1969, page 37.

on desegregation, the board decided to hold a public referendum. In that vote, freedom of choice was defeated by seventy-one to twenty-nine percent. Why? It is fair to conclude that the major fear of white parents had been removed by the educational accomplishment guarantee.[16]

Texarkana may hold other lessons for us, but it is only the first in what we hope will be a long series of projects. The concepts of accountability and educational engineering are catching the imagination of a broad audience, including school officials, educators in a variety of corporations and non-profit centers, and leaders at the highest levels of government. With roots deep in American traditions of enterprise, responsiveness, and flexibility, these concepts are now nurturing a movement in education that will probably affect all of us.

16. Here the author is relying not only on an analysis by Charles Blaschke, in a letter dated February 5, 1970, but also on the article by Richard A. Bumstead, already cited.

The
Movement
for
Accountability

Chapter 7

T HE MOVEMENT FOR ACCOUNTABILITY in public education arises not from any single source but from the shared experience of many of us who work in or for the schools. In urging the need for accountability in speeches throughout 1969, the author found that many leaders, in politics as well as in education, welcomed this concept on the basis of their own observations. Many spoke in favor of accountability, and after the Texarkana program had begun, leaders elsewhere began to commit themselves, in various ways, to the new concept.

Endorsing the Concept of Accountability

The agreement between the Board of Education of the City of New York and the teachers' union highlights the goal of accountability in its preamble. Under the word *accountability* in large boldface type the agreement states:

> The Board of Education and the Union recognize that the major problem of our school system is the failure to educate *all* of our students and the massive academic retardation which exists especially among minority group students. The Board and the Union therefore agree to join in an effort, in cooperation with universities, community school boards and parent organizations, to seek solutions to this major problem and to develop objective criteria of professional accountability.[1]

In December 1969, for example, the superintendent of schools in San Francisco announced that, in order to pursue a "zero reject" program, he was "seeking accountability contracts from publishers who will bid on learning package materials and consultant services with accountability provisions which provide that the publisher will be paid on the basis of the successful student achievement of pre-negotiated standards of performance." The

1. The contract is called "Agreement between the Board of Education of the City of New York and the United Federation of Teachers, AFL-CIO, covering day school classroom teachers and per session teachers for the period September 8, 1969 to September 8, 1972."

superintendent made clear that such contracts "would provide that full payment for the materials would be made for only those students who showed a full year's growth after being in the program for that period."[2]

In mid-January 1970, Jesse Unruh, Democratic Assembly Leader in California, introduced a bill to adopt educational engineering widely in that state. He called for opening the schools to help from the private sector, noting that "one of the problems facing the public education system . . . is that it has no real competitors to spur it to excellence." Under the bill, California schools could negotiate performance contracts with private educational firms for reading and math programs. The firms would be reimbursed only if they met the agreed standards. In meeting the contention that performance contracts are "overly businesslike," Unruh noted that his bill "has the great advantage of fixing responsibility for results and places a new and badly needed emphasis on the achievement of children in the basic skills."[3]

On January 20, 1970, the superintendent of schools in San Diego issued a forceful policy statement for his district, declaring that "the school system must be accountable for . . . educational results"; that "programs and practices must be designed so that they can be evaluated in terms of educational outcomes as this relates to program costs"; that "the people have a right to know all possible information about the needs, problems, successes, and failures of the public schools"; that "the business and industrial community must be given an opportunity to contribute their expertise to the educational institution"; and that evaluation of programs "must be, in the final analysis, supervised by experts who are free of any bias." Above all, he emphasized "accountability to the people."[4]

A week later the concept of accountability turned up in Chicago, where the superintendent of schools released, for the first time, school-by-school results on tests of achievement in reading and math. Headlined in the local press, this report showed that

2. Dr. Robert E. Jenkins, "Educational Equality/Quality," a report by the superintendent, December 12, 1969, page 22.

3. UPI story, datelined Sacramento, California, as printed in *The Times* of San Mateo, California, January 19, 1970.

4. Statement from the Office of the Superintendent, San Diego City Schools, January 20, 1970, page 1.

white schools, in general, had markedly higher test scores than black schools and that the average for all schools was not only below national norms, but further below than ever before. In releasing these figures, the superintendent explained that "we have to be accountable for our stewardship of the children entrusted to us." He added that the board of education may begin judging school principals on how well their students learn, declaring that performance appraisal of this kind is "a dangerous idea, but we have to do it." A member of the board of education was quoted as saying that "we need results from our efforts, and we should know why if we don't get the results"; and another member said that the release of data would generate "pressures which are needed from various areas of the city."[5]

In speaking to the American Association of School Administrators on February 14, 1970. James E. Allen, the former U.S. Commissioner of Education, said that what has generated disillusionment and a lack of confidence in the public schools is "in large measure our inability to substantiate results." Calling for research aimed at improving the ability to assess the effectiveness of educational programs, he declared that "the strengthening of the concept of accountability . . . is imperative."[6]

On March 3, 1970, President Nixon sent a special message on educational reform to Congress. Along with other proposals, he called upon the school systems to "begin the responsible, open measurement of how well the educational process is working" and he firmly endorsed the concept of accountability:

> School administrators and school teachers alike are responsible for their performance, and it is in their interest as well as in the interests of their pupils that they be held accountable. Success should be measured not by some fixed national norm, but rather by the results achieved in relation to the actual situation of the particular school and the particular set of pupils.[7]

The president distinguished carefully between local accountability and what he called the "bugaboo" of national standards. He observed that, in fact, "there has never been any serious effort to

5. Peter Negronida, "Redmond Says He May Judge His Aids on How Pupils Learn," *Chicago Tribune*, January 29, 1970, page 8.

6. Speech by James E. Allen, Jr., as reported in the *Washington Post*, February 15, 1970.

7. This passage and others from the special message can be found among excerpts published in the *New York Times*, March 4, 1970, page 28.

impose national standards on educational programs," adding that "if we act wisely in this generation we can be reasonably confident that no such effort will arise in future generations." He further stated that:

> In opposing some mythical threat what we have too often been doing is avoiding accountability for our own local performance. We have, as a nation, too long avoided thinking of the productivity of schools. This is a mistake because it undermines the principle of local control of education. Ironic though it is, the avoidance of accountability is the single most serious threat to a continued and even more pluralistic educational system.

By the time this message was written, the concept of accountability had been endorsed and explored not only by the officials and writers quoted above and in chapter six, but also by an encouraging variety of other sources. For example, in September 1969, Dr. James S. Coleman had recommended "the publication of carefully designed measures of academic performance, which pay attention both to the total distribution of achievement and to the increment in achievement rather than the absolute level."[8] Without data such as this, accountability is impossible; but in place of relatively primitive tests now widely used, we must develop measures that are increasingly relevant and reliable.

Using such measures, we could discover the educational results being produced by various school personnel. In November 1969, a leading U.S. bank published a report on the New York City schools, airing the argument that "the most important attribute of a principal or teacher should not be whether he is liked by his superiors, his peers or even the community, but whether he is able to elicit satisfactory improvement from the children he teaches."[9] This report suggested that instead of administering all programs for compensatory education through the central bureaucracy, the funds "could be put to good advantage by providing principals of disadvantaged schools with discretionary funds to use for whatever special purposes they themselves deem necessary to improve achievement levels in their schools." Although the report acknowledged the difficulty of measuring achievement, it argued that if we allow the principals the necessary discretion we can also hold them correspondingly "accountable."

8. James S. Coleman, "Incentives in American Education," *Educate*, September 1969, page 19.

9. First National City Bank, New York, "Public Education in New York City," November 1969, pages 33-34.

Also in November 1969, an educational publishing firm announced that it would sell materials for a reading program under an accountability contract. If a class advanced one grade level within the nine months of the school year, the firm would keep the full price paid for their books and other materials, but for each month the class as a whole fell short of the full grade level, the publisher would reimburse the school for ten percent of the price. Achievement would be measured by "any of the nationally recognized reading tests" and the guarantee would apply not to individual students but to the average of the class. In order for the school to get a rebate, it would have to show that all students in the class had completed their workbook exercises, as well as a minimum of twelve "composition cycles."[10]

In January 1970, the distinguished educator Kenneth B. Clark called for "a system of accountability . . . to insure that each teacher is responsible to his principal or assistant principal for the reading achievement of the children in his class"; and the principal, in turn, to the assistant superintendent or some other supervisor. In this scheme, as in others previously mentioned, the performance of school personnel is measured primarily not by observations of their work but rather by their "performance . . . as this is reflected in the academic performance of their students."[11]

The San Diego Accountability Project
Negotiations for a different kind of accountability were announced that same month by the San Diego city schools, which became the first urban district to follow the example of Texarkana and work out a performance contract with a private firm. Beginning in fall 1970, the contractor, Educational Development Laboratory, will run a reading program for 9,600 elementary students now reading below grade level. The program will involve 195 teachers at six San Diego schools where the students are mostly from minority groups. The contractor will receive $1.4 million if it reduces reading disabilities by twenty-five percent the first year, fifty percent the second year, and brings all students up to grade level the third year. The district hopes to receive federal funds for the program under Title III of the Elementary and Secondary School Act, and if the grant is forthcoming, the contractor will provide equipment,

10. Press release, Open Court Publishing Co., La Salle, Illinois, November 21, 1969.

11. Kenneth B. Clark, "Answer for 'Disadvantaged' Is Effective Teaching," *New York Times*, January 12, 1970.

supplies, materials, consultation service, and in-service training for the regular San Diego teachers who will staff the program.[12]

Further Reactions to Accountability

In late January 1970, accountability and performance contracting, exemplified by the experiment in Texarkana and the newly announced San Diego program, were the subject of intensive discussion at the 1970 National Laboratory for the Advancement of Education, which drew an estimated 3,000 participants. According to an analysis in the *Washington Post*, this "new, hardheaded approach to upgrading the nation's schools" was already winning adherents not only within the "learning industry," but also among educators and education planners. "A growing number are becoming more receptive toward the management know-how as well as the products of modern industrial technology," said the report, adding that some "even see promise in harnessing the profit motive in the cause of boosting classroom performance."[13]

In February 1970, the editor of *Instructor* magazine stated that after the heavy federal investment in education, "now it is entirely proper for the public to demand some evaluation of what has been accomplished." Drawing an analogy between investors seeking a "fair return" and legislators appropriating funds for the schools, he noted that the lawmakers "must provide their constituents with proof of a fair return on their investments in education" and that "all of us in the schools are being held accountable — in other words, responsible for providing the evidence to justify increased government investment in education."[14]

Means for providing the results as well as evidence of them were featured at the eighth annual conference of the National Committee for Support of the Public Schools, held in late March 1970. Under the theme of "how to change the system," vigorous panel discussions focused on such means as accountability, performance contracting, and educational technology.[15] The widespread interest in these areas was marked, too, by requests for

12. See *Education U.S.A.*, February 2, 1970, page 122.

13. Eric Wentworth, "Profit Motive Harnessed in New School Experiment," *Washington Post*, February 2, 1970.

14. "Accountability," an editorial, *Instructor*, February, 1970, page 6.

15. Among the other topics were decentralization, voucher schemes, and "alternative systems of education."

information that the U.S. Office of Education had received from more than 250 school districts and by a number of thoughtful, comprehensive newspaper stories. For example, the *Washington Post* reported that, if administration plans succeed, the 1970s will become the "Age of Accountability" in American education. If so, said the article:

> Private "learning companies" will be a stronger force in bringing about more effective schooling; school systems all over the country will set new, more meaningful goals for students; schools will be rated on whether their students attain these goals — rather than just on the classrooms, equipment, textbooks and teachers they provide; school programs will also be judged on relative cost effectiveness; [and] a new professional, the "independent accomplishment auditor" will play a key role in these ratings.[16]

And in May 1970 the Office of Economic Opportunity announced a multi-million dollar one-year experiment in accountability. Their program will include twelve to fifteen thousand students in twenty-four school districts around the nation.

Who Is Accountable?

If this chapter were a history of the early acceptance of accountability we could add other expressions of support, but the quotations already given are enough to suggest the range and intensity of interest in the concept. Even in this sampling of statements, however, we find that "accountability" and similar words are being used in a variety of ways. In order to sort out the usages, we ought to keep asking *who* is supposed to be accountable *to whom.*

For example, are we talking about teachers being accountable to their principals? Kenneth Clark, in the brief excerpt we quoted, used the word in this sense. Do we mean that principals are to be accountable to their superintendents? This was proposed not only by Clark, but by the bank's report and by the superintendent in Chicago. Or perhaps we mean that the school system is accountable to the general public? This usage was evident in the speech by Commissioner Allen, in the release of test data by Chicago, in the *Instructor* magazine editorial, and in the policy statement by San Diego. The word *accountability* is also used to describe a relationship between a private contractor and a school district, as in

16. Eric Wentworth, "An 'Age of Accountability' Is Sought for U.S. Education," *Washington Post*, March 30, 1970, page A2.

the Texarkana program, the bill introduced by Unruh, the San Diego contract negotiations, and in speeches by the author. Under this last form of accountability, contracts can range from the supply of instructional materials alone, as in the money-back guarantee from an educational publisher, all the way to the operation of an entire instructional program, as in Texarkana.

Some of these usages refer to relations within the school system itself; and another, to relations between the system as a whole and its constituency. To some degree, these relations of accountability have always existed. In the early nineteenth century and perhaps at other times in American history, teachers in certain schools simply were not paid unless their students could pass muster. For example, in the 1817 Georgia law applying to "poor schools" (the adjective was supposed to apply to the income of families, not to the quality of the instructional program), the commissioners were forbidden to pay a teacher *any* salary if an examination showed that his students had not made good progress in that quarter.[17] Similarly, superintendents can be fired, and school board members voted out of office.

Positive Incentives for Accountability

Although schools, like other systems, may require negative sanctions as a last resort, educational engineering relies more heavily on positive incentives. In fact, we argue that the schools now suffer because they offer so few incentives to anybody. As noted in chapter three, we would use development capital not only to support new programs, but to reward those who plan and staff programs that satisfy performance criteria. We point out that, apart from the issue of salary bonuses, the opportunity to translate good ideas into local practice is often the most powerful incentive of all. And in all of this, we insist that no group or official can properly be held accountable unless he is given the discretion and means to conduct a program in the form he has planned or approved. In other words, in order to make someone answer for his stewardship, we must first give him the necessary funds and, within appropriate limits, the freedom to use them according to his best judgment.

In considering any plan for having one party answer to another, we must ask not only what are the penalties for failure, but—much

17. *Georgia Education Law* (Atlanta: The Harrison Co., Publishers, 1965).

more important — what are the opportunities for success. In considering the relation between teachers and the school system, for example, we should think much less in terms of firing or somehow penalizing slow teachers than of rewarding and assisting the more successful ones. Thus we can respect union agreements concerning tenure and basic pay scales, while also opening the system to the beneficial effects of various forms of incentives and opportunities for more satisfying work. After all, once minimum standards of working conditions are met, how could we improve those conditions more meaningfully than by offering teachers a stake in improving the school? As educational technology improves, unions will face a choice between regressive featherbedding contracts that could stifle innovation, and leadership toward reforms so that union members can help to pioneer in the development of new, more satisfying schools. If they choose the second path, unions will press for the widespread use of educational engineering and for the opportunities it can help to open for teachers as well as for students.

Seen from within the school system, the concept of accountability thus means that the staff at all levels can expect new power to innovate, for without it how could they fairly be held to answer for results? Seen from the viewpoint of a taxpayer, accountability means that voters can insist on having the data on educational results, so that claims can be matched against performance, and on setting aside a portion of education funds as development capital, so that we have a source of innovations to measure the rest of the program against.

Linking Results to Resources

In a nutshell, we are saying that accountability is not a sudden, harsh demand for results from a system that is given no new means to produce them, but rather part of a feedback loop through which results are linked to resources as in any cycle. The two are linked at both ends: in the absence of results from a given program, we would invest future development capital elsewhere, but in order for a program to show what it can do, we must first supply the resources it needs.

This feedback loop is especially direct in the relationship between a school and a private firm. No responsible firm would accept a contract unless it had the means to do what was necessary.

Conversely, would a school system sign a second contract with a firm if it had done badly on the first, or if another firm offers a better program? And the firm is directly accountable at the end of a program, for in a performance contract its earnings depend on the educational results.

In the relationship between a school and a contracting firm the accountability might be called strict, whereas in the relationship between a school board and its constituency, for example, the accountability is somewhat loose. In a school board election, the timing and the issues are not strictly linked to a particular program: sometimes voters seem to be swayed most strongly by a loosely defined controversy, by a general sense of how well the schools are doing, or by distorted images of the candidates. The value of individual programs usually disappears in the confusion. Under a performance contract, however, nothing is at stake *except* a particular program. Accountability here is strict, not only in its limitation to a single program, but also in its dependence on clearly defined performance criteria. In the management of the public schools, both forms of accountability can play valuable roles, so long as we do not confuse them.[18]

We have argued that whenever accountability is required, a capability must also be provided or enlisted. Thus, as we seek to make various elements of the educational complex answer for their programs, we must simultaneously ask how each element can be empowered to do what is asked of it. In the case of elements within the school system, the rigidity of structures may sometimes hinder or even prevent the development of new capabilities. There are many ways, so far little used, for increasing the flexibility even of severely burdened systems. In chapter three, for example, we discussed the role of development capital used within (as well as outside) the school system itself. But whenever internal rigidity blocks the improvement of educational programs, or when needs call for methods new to the system, we ought to be able to enlist outside help.

Performance contracts are not the only means for securing spe-

18. One form of accountability has even come to the Ivy League. "At the urging of Kingman Brewster Jr., a committee of trustees has been selected to review his tenure as president of Yale University," reported the *New York Times*, March 15, 1970. Noting that traditionally the president of Yale, as of most other universities, serves an indefinite term, the article stated that "last fall Mr. Brewster recommended that Yale adopt a new policy of 'accountability' to guard against 'incompetent and unresponsive administration.'"

cial assistance, but they offer several advantages: (1) as an outside agency, a firm in the education business can bring to the district not only a fresh approach, but also certain kinds of talent and technology not usually found in the schools, along with the experience of having worked in other districts; (2) a business firm will go to some lengths to do an exemplary job because its profits depend on the reputation for results that it can establish and sustain; and (3) in case of a failure, an outside firm is paid a reduced fee and is easy to get rid of, whereas a program started within the bureaucracy may languish for years.

Developing Capability for Accountability

To retrace the steps of our discussion: in order to gain the advantages of accountability, we must develop or enlist the capability to do what is required. Among the ways of enlisting outside capability, performance contracts offer important advantages; and once we seek to employ this method of contracting, we also need the other main parts of educational engineering. In order to plan the program and pay the bills we need development capital. In order to coordinate local needs, federal grants management, and the offerings of the education industry, the schools need management support. And in order to measure the results, upon which payment depends, we need a mutually acceptable accomplishment auditor. One step leads to the next.

How can these various elements be put to work? What we have so far is a widespread acceptance of the concept of accountability, an outline for the process of educational engineering, and a few pioneering performance contracts. Where do we go from here? Early experience suggests that if government provides the incentives, and if supporters of educational engineering offer some coordination, private firms will respond very quickly and intensively.

The Federal Role

First, then, what can the federal government do to help? The Office of Education can, under the leadership of its commissioner and of the president, take such steps as the following:

(1) Require or encourage the use of performance contracts wherever existing legislation allows it, so that the results sought

can be measured, and schools can obtain the necessary outside services.

(2) Seek new legislation that provides for a three-stage funding process similar to the process outlined in the dropout prevention amendment authored by Senator George Murphy. Ideally, a preliminary proposal from a school district would lead to a planning grant, with which the district would work out a request for proposal. Firms would prepare detailed bids and the one chosen by the district would become the formal proposal sent to the U.S. Office of Education, which, upon approval, would announce a grant. After the district had engaged an independent accomplishment auditor, the school would receive the actual program grant and could begin promptly.

(3) Prepare a contractor capability catalog in which school districts could find accurate descriptions of firms and non-profit agencies in such fields as systems design, management support, instructional hardware, in-service training, program operation, and accomplishment auditing. Also prepare a manual of procedures for educational engineering or, more narrowly, performance contracting.

(4) "Develop broader and more sensitive measurements of learning than we now have," to quote the special message on educational reform that the president issued in March 1970. In that message, he said that in working on these measurements, we should "pay as much heed to what are called the 'immeasurables' of schooling (largely because no one has yet learned to measure them), such as responsibility, wit, and humanity, as it does to verbal and mathematical achievement." Meanwhile, however, we might keep in mind that nobody would dream of posing "wit" or "humanity" as a performance criterion; and that for the relatively modest purposes of educational engineering, we do need to work very hard on measurements of reading, for example.

(5) As a larger federal budget for education becomes available, which ought to be soon, devote a substantial share of it to performance contracting, a form that both ensures local control and enlists the widest possible range of outside assistance within the process of bidding.

The Role of the Educational Engineer
Along with federal initiatives, educational engineering needs its own organizational form, perhaps a professional society, which will

bring together the growing number of people who would like to contribute to this field. If such a society is not organized by educators, others will probably take the initiative.

How has this field grown? With the advent of massive federal aid to education, the business of changing the public schools to meet new social priorities began in earnest. Like agriculture, business, and medicine before it, the educational enterprise began to call on an array of new talent representing a mix of disciplines not always found in universities. Thus, over the past decade, an increasing amount of money in education has gone to people with expertise in such fields as systems design and analysis (for "management by objectives"), quality control, operations research, instructional technology, facilities design, performance contracting, and accomplishment auditing. Taken together, these interrelated fields represent an early form of educational engineering. Coupled with the traditional emphasis on humanistic values and knowledge from the behavioral sciences, educational engineering might assist strongly in the reform, renewal, and enhancement of our schools. Without this new field, where could we go for the skills on which we must draw in order to translate the variety of demands now upon us into viable, effective programs?

A society of educational engineers will do essentially what any professional society does: develop or review training programs, set standards of performance and of ethics, sponsor and disseminate research, and provide a meeting ground for its members and those who work with them. In the formation of the society, we ought to seek a balance between the development of specialized capabilities and the clarification of educational needs as felt not only by teachers and officials in our schools, but also by our ultimate "consumer," the student. In the growth of educational engineering, we must always remember that unless our purpose is clear, special skills alone could lead us astray.

In this chapter we have briefly reviewed the movement for accountability in public education, traced some of its immediate implications and set forth a few proposals for what we can do next. In chapter eight we will move on to a consideration of its broader political and educational meaning, including such issues as the "new federalism," patterns of desegregation, the crisis of authority, voucher schemes, instructional technology, wider roles for teachers, and limitations of the process outlined in this book.

Implications
of the
New Alliance

68/27

Chapter 8

TODAY WE ARE CONSTANTLY HEARING about student unrest, not only in the colleges, but increasingly in high schools. What is causing it? Is it the growth of a counter-culture based in part on drugs, immediacy of goals, distrust of elders, and personal involvement and freedom? Is it opposition to the war, or disillusionment with the establishment? To accept any of these explanations as the whole story is to miss the yearning of many young people to make our institutions work. What these students oppose is not the existence of institutions such as schools, but the incompetence and irrelevance that they sometimes display.

Boredom in Our Schools

Many students, when asked what is their dominant feeling in school, answer with a single word: boredom. What could be more dehumanizing? Most of us can still recall the extraordinary dreariness of so much of the teaching to which we were exposed: the textbooks flat as old root beer, the boring assignments, the perfunctory explanations, the passive note taking, the mindless regurgitation of meaningless facts, and a scheme of grading that taught so many children to give up hope. Our schools have made some progress in these areas, but we have a long way to go. In many classrooms these boring practices still occur. As the president said in his special message on educational reform, "We now have reason to believe that young people may be learning much more outside school than they learn in school." Is it any wonder? Young people almost swim in a mixture of media such as magazines and paperback books, recorded music, TV, and easy travel. They are

123

exposed to a life that is exciting and exhilarating. They are eager to do, learn, taste, see.

What they are *not* eager to do is to serve time, to sit in a room as the world is sliced up into little units that teacher serves up according to an invariable curriculum. How often do they slip away into half-sleep or escape to a world of daydreams? How many look forward solely to recess, snow days, and social get-togethers? If we were to sit through a typical school week as if we were students, with no hope of escape, we might begin to appreciate the terrible effects of boredom, redundancy, endless repetition.

The students are restless.

Some people have always replied that learning to read, for example, is hard work and thus bound to be tedious. Without for a moment agreeing, we can ask what happens when the instructional program in reading is not only tedious but ineffective. In this case, the student is cheated cruelly. If he becomes a troublemaker we define him as a kind of social threat, but if he lapses into peaceful tedium we may easily forget about him. Does either of these reactions really deal with the problem?

Passing the Buck

Ineffective institutions tend to blame others and are blamed in return. In classical fashion the buck is passed. The society says to its schools, "Why are you falling down on the job?" And distraught school officials reply, "If only you knew our problems," and ask "Why are the kids so poorly motivated?" When somebody fails, he becomes defined as "bad." Teachers refer to "bad students," parents to "bad schools," thus confusing an incapability with a kind of moral stigma. In place of this demonology we might consider Banfield's analysis that is no less relevant to education than to government:

> In judging how a political system will work over time, increases in the burdens upon it are obviously extremely relevant. They are not all that must be considered, however. Changes in the "capability" of a system, that is, in its ability to manage conflict and to impose settlements, are equally relevant. The "effectiveness" of a political system is a ratio between burdens and capability. Even though the burdens upon it increase, the effectiveness of a system will also increase if there is a sufficient accompanying increase in capability. Similarly, even though there

is an increase in capability, the effectiveness of a system will decrease if there is a more than commensurate increase in burdens.[1]

The Educational Engineering Approach

Instead of blaming the schools or seeking a secret flaw within them, educational engineering simply assumes that, because of changes in our cultural expectations and of larger social problems, many schools are now overburdened. To the extent that a school is ineffective, we assume that it needs to develop a further capability in certain areas.

Educational engineering exists to supply specific capabilities to our schools. It is thus an alternative to the present stalemate between schools that literally do not know how to change except in trivial or belated ways, and certain critics who, in the course of pointing out many flaws, demand that there be a total change. If there were no middle ground between excuses called forth by incapacity and the guidance of utopian visions, we would surely be in trouble. But as schools come to be held more strictly accountable, they are going to recognize their need for outside help. Right now they are a bit defensive about things outside, because most of what comes in is abusive.

How can schools learn to draw on outside help? As we learn to use educational engineering, schools will work out a variety of flexible alliances with sources of development capital, management support, instructional programs, and accomplishment audits. Imagine a lone, struggling builder faced with restricted funds, novel and demanding specifications, and harsh conditions on the site. What if he suddenly had the benefit of an "angel" who provided funds for the necessary technology, consultants on management skills and engineering, and construction experts who could demonstrate new methods in the field? This would be similar to the variety of help educational engineering can provide. Through this process, a school can determine its goals in measurable terms, discover how to obtain and coordinate the assistance it needs, arrange for one outside agency to introduce a new program and for

1. Edward C. Banfield, "The Political Implications of Metropolitan Growth," *Daedalus*, Winter 1961, page 60.

another to assess the results, and then, if results are good, adopt the innovations easily as part of their regular services.

Results. That is what educational engineering is all about.

We believe that schools will achieve results neither through more of the same nor through surrendering to reactionary or utopian criticism. Instead, we propose a middle way.

This middle way runs through several areas, including the relationship of the federal government to the schools, of schools to private industry, and of schools to their constituents. Let us consider these critical areas one by one.

The Federal Role

In proposing a proper relationship between Washington and local schools, some educators would like to centralize as large a percentage as possible of our total spending on education. They feel that instead of allowing thousands of inexperienced local boards or antiquated state agencies to perpetuate a failing system, we ought to filter more of the education budget through a relatively small elite. Other educators and politicians go to the opposite extreme, saying that since citizens feel powerless to influence a remote governing body, we ought simply to turn over a substantial share of federal taxes to lower levels of government, for use in education and in other fields. Through educational engineering, however, we can take advantage of both of these ideas, calling on the federal government to sponsor research, disseminate information, and provide development capital, while the local boards are left free to invest the funds within a rich variety of available services that are tied to local goals through performance contracts. As we noted in chapter three, the trick is to distinguish between *kinds* of money, instead of talking as if all money in education were used for one purpose. Once we distinguish among money for research, for installation of workable programs, and for their continued operation, we can assign these various functions to the levels of government most suited to them and thus dissolve a stark ideological dispute into a practical arrangement.

The Role of Private Industry

The same process applies to the relationship between schools and private enterprise. Some educators are automatically suspicious of any proposal for opening the schools to assistance from a firm (or, in some cases, even from a non-profit institution). They feel both that asking for help implies an admission of defeat, and that allowing somebody to make a profit on the children's education is somehow wrong. After all, educators are trained to provide a service: if they have to call on others, why hire them in the first place?

In view of the history and sociology of education, these views are understandable, but are they still relevant? In education we like to describe ourselves as professionals, but the refusal to make use of outside aid is not a mark of a professional. Where would doctors be without drugs, instruments, and all the skills that go into designing and maintaining a hospital? Where would they be without intensive medical research? Yet none of these are, in general, provided by practicing physicians. Should we be any less willing to collaborate with others in education?

The issue of profits deflects us from the real issue, which is service. In every case we ought to be asking *who* can provide a given service effectively, and at what price. Like doctors, school officials have long bought many items and services from private industry. Apart from the school building itself and the many supplies, we buy millions of dollars worth of instructional materials, now mainly textbooks. Why not extend the same principle to programs of instruction?

Some critics of the public schools want to extend this principle much, much further. Through a voucher plan, they want to allow parents to send their children to any supplier of educational services, either public or private, and if private, either a school or a learning center run by a firm. If our better public school teachers were hired away by a variety of corporations, what would be left? How could the public schools possibly compete? And, as some would add, if they would be unable to compete, why should they exist?

Again, educational engineering offers a middle way. As soon as educators learn to manage the array of assistance available to them, and harness private enterprise to the goals of the schools instead of leaving it to compete against the schools, we can achieve a set of results that appear to be impossible both in the unassisted public school and in the free-for-all inspired by a voucher scheme. While preserving the common schools, we can bring into them all the variety, talent, and flexibility available throughout our society. In place of a closed educational system, we can fashion an open one.

The Role of the Community

The same principle holds in the relationship of the schools to our society (or, in particular, to the local community). Some educators seem to want to run a sort of monolithic system in which the public is told to leave it to the experts. Parents are told, with a petulance that varies inversely with their social class, that nobody can say anything useful about a process so complex as education unless they have taken the necessary courses. Meanwhile, the PTA is supposed to sell cookies and support the professionals.

Today, however, we are getting tired of expertise and in some cases rejecting it summarily. To an extraordinary degree, the general populace seems disenchanted with the elite who supposedly lead the masses. Our society has discovered, with as much anxiety as glee, that presidents and professors, bankers and parents and policemen are quite as capable as the young or the ignorant in making fools of themselves.

In family life, we see this disenchantment as a revolt by many young people against parental views, as a rejection of the age-old claim to superior knowledge or wisdom. We see many business school graduates dismissing commerce as dull and uninspiring in comparison with opportunities for social service. In domestic affairs, especially in education, we see poor people demanding a voice in shaping programs that affect them. Across the spectrum of national concerns we hear a new cry for participatory democracy, and people long docile are learning how to make themselves heard. In the school systems we hear a rash of demands for participation in decision making: teacher power, student power, black power, parent power, and (in the fast-wilting phrase) flower power.

Using the Specialist

In the face of these demands, some educators act as if we have only two choices: either defend our prerogatives to run the schools according to our professional wisdom, or throw open the process of governance to a populist chaos in which every citizen claims expertise about education on the grounds of having gone through school or of having a child there. Is there no middle way?

Let me propose an analogy from medical practice. If an injured person brought to an emergency ward needs immediate care but has to lie there for several hours before he gets it, we would all charge the medical staff with sheer incompetence. In demanding improvement, we would all feel well within the layman's proper sphere of criticism. We are not invading the physician's professional domain, but simply claiming that an institution should meet the human needs it was established to serve. On the other hand, we respect the special skills of a surgeon based on his years of education and experience and his reputation for results. We do not dash into an operating room and say, "Look here, I'm just as American as you are, and this is a democratic country: give me the scalpel and let me remove that appendix."

Similarly, educators must respond effectively to the legitimate demands of their constituents. A school is supposed to teach such basic skills as reading. If it fails, parents and other critics have no less right to demand a change than the layman in our analogy of the emergency room. To a somewhat greater extent than in an operating room, these critics of the schools may even have ideas about how the problem might be solved; but in each case the professional has to do the work himself. If a surgeon needed technical help, he would consult not a layman but a specialist.

In educational engineering we also call on the specialist, and in many cases we find the necessary help organized within a private firm. In order to respond to the rightful demands of our constituents while remaining in charge of the schools, we call on the services we need, knowing that enthusiasm for extreme forms of participatory democracy reflects less a desire to do the work of running schools than a need to see educational results instead of excuses; and knowing, too, that the test of a profession is not whether it provides every service from within but whether it can harness available services in order to produce a satisfying result.

Citizens are right to insist that schools as well as other public institutions be responsive. After all, schools exist not to provide careers for educators, but to educate our children. When a program fails, however, we need a wider choice than the one between gilding the failure with more tax money and damning educators as a pack of fools. In order to extend the capabilities of the schools, we need, most of all, to open them to a wide variety of outside assistance. The day of the closed educational system is waning, for seldom can a closed system manage to renew itself: without help it lacks the perspective, the motive, the resources, and the methods necessary for adaptation.

Possibilities for Improving Education

In adapting to new demands, our schools need the benefits of more research on learning, as the president noted in his special message on educational reform; but we must not defer action, or the means to support it, until the day when we may finally understand "the mystery of the learning process."[2] The fact is that we already know a great deal more than we are putting into practice. On the basis of careful studies and voluminous reports, generated by the billions of federal dollars spent recently on education, we have many examples of favorable opportunities for improving school productivity:

(1) Elementary schools where children are allowed considerable choice of what each person wants to study within a rich environment, a safe microcosm of the world outside;

(2) Schools where great emphasis is placed on older children tutoring younger ones, and where community service is encouraged and properly managed;

(3) Schools in which each child sets his own pace in working through individually prescribed instruction;

(4) Work-study schools that provide a link between education and the world outside by offering part-time classroom education to young people who are meanwhile also learning on the job;

(5) Other types of schools with emphasis on learning outside the classroom, with visits to museums, factories, libraries, farms, and hospitals; or with televised instruction at home or in school;

(6) Schools where parents or students or members of the community or all of them actively participate in planning the program of the school; and

(7) Competitive programs within a school, or schools within a public system, arranged so that students may choose among alternative ways of reaching similar goals.

Each of these examples indicates a kind of responsiveness, and in each of these schools the work of the educator, as of the student, is more satisfying and absorbing then in the many institutions that fail to meet the needs of their people.

The Limitations of Educational Engineering

So far we have traced the path of the "middle way" provided by

2. *New York Times*, March 4, 1970, page 28.

educational engineering. We have seen how it avoids extremes in the relationship of schools to the federal government, to private enterprise, and to the local community. Compared with many current proposals for educational reform, the process outlined in this book offers a relatively moderate method for increasing the capabilities of overburdened schools. The process is orderly, flexible, and modest: instead of making promises, we emphasize results.

In tracing the elements of educational engineering we have deliberately suggested several limitations on its use. For example, this process ought to be applied only to skills we can measure within a tolerable range of accuracy and reliability. Hopefully, as our ability to measure educational accomplishment increases, so will the applicability of the process. Initially, though, we ought to exclude educational engineering from areas of learning that still either bewilder test makers or call for an amount or kind of testing that would disrupt the instructional program or direct it away from larger goals and toward an attempt to "teach the exam." Just as with any new process that releases much-needed energies, we will probably be tempted to extend the application of educational engineering faster than its own development will properly allow. At each stage, therefore, we ought to inquire whether we have the means both to supply an instructional program and to test the results. In the first stage, we ought to focus on guaranteeing what the U.S. Commissioner of Education has called "the right to read."[3] Even in dealing with such an elementary skill as reading, we need much better instruments for measuring achievement. Many of the standardized tests, which still include some of the pioneers in this field, call for substantial improvement; and the movement for accountability and performance contracting will undoubtedly create a market for newly developed instruments as well.

Another prudent limitation on the scope of educational engineering applies to the practice of auditing. In theory, the independent educational accomplishment auditor could review not only test scores but the methods of the program, its management, and the workings of the school itself. He could range as widely as a management consultant would in reviewing a firm's operations. A school might welcome such a broad report if the auditor were allowed to observe carefully and to analyze practices in management or teaching as skillfully as we give tests and interpret scores.

3. Former U.S. Commissioner of Education, James E. Allen, Jr., September 1969.

We can train auditors in these wider, demanding tasks, but until a group of highly trained and experienced auditors is widely available, perhaps we ought to ask the educational auditors to limit their work mainly to supplying reliable data on student performance and achievement.

In the first period of educational engineering, we ought likewise to limit what we ask of private enterprise. Firms in the education business have access to technology, capital, staff, and consultants on which the average school could not dream of drawing except through performance contracts; but even after some spectacular successes, we must not expect miracles. A firm is only as good as the instructional program it can provide. Educational goals differ. So do local conditions. Some firms have a head start in certain areas because of work for federal programs such as the Job Corps and aspects of military training, but programs designed to teach reading to nineteen-year-olds in the army may not work when used with twelve-year-olds in the schools. Similarly, the ability to furnish a successful reading program for a certain grade range does not guarantee that a firm in the education industry can duplicate its success at another level, much less for another subject. Apart from a measure of caution in dealing with a largely unknown industry, we ought to expect a period of some turbulence as the firms and their programs are sorted out. What makes the experimentation possible for the schools is the mechanism of the performance contract. If a particular contractor fails to some extent, the school will be able to lower his fee or require him to continue without pay, or both, until the job is done. And since performance results are quickly known, school officials will soon have a firm basis for judging future bids.

The Benefits of Educational Engineering

What benefits does this process offer? Let us consider in turn its potential for students, for teachers, and for administrators. Since educational engineering is an approach broader than any particular program, it will soon affect the way students view their own process of learning. For example, most classes now begin with a vague preview of the material to be covered and consist of a series of assignments, review sessions, and tests. There is nothing much to look forward to. In contrast, most successful commercial enterprises promote their products and services in such a way as to arouse interest before the consumer uses them. We read attractive brochures of a foreign country and begin thinking about a trip; or we study the investment pages and contemplate the purchase of some stocks; or we hear about a new kind of skis and decide to try them. The actual experience of using the product or owning it is positively enhanced by our advance knowledge and anticipation of it.

Student Benefits

In schools, however, where do students go to find out what is being offered? Most of them enter courses with little notion of what they will study. Little attempt is made to build prior interest in, or to prepare students for, the experience. Why not give them a prospectus setting out the intellectual adventure they are undertaking? We could list the things they will learn, the books they will read, ideas they will encounter, and a sample of the assignments they will have. Properly done, such a prospectus would arouse intellectual ambition in the students and help their parents understand what is going on.

Any school could do this, but the link to educational engineering is plain. If the process of innovation requires school officials to define their goals in operational terms as a first step, the school will be able to share with students not merely airy objectives, such as "the ability to communicate effectively," but specific sets of skills. In fact, we will know that the spirit of educational engineering has reached our students when, instead of saying "I've *had* that" (meaning a course), they begin to say "I can *do* that" (meaning a task). Education is less a program of material to be gone through than a set of skills to master; and that is the way we ought to treat it in planning.

Teacher Benefits

Educational engineering offers teachers a wider role. When farmers had nothing more than a horse and a plow their productivity was limited by their lack of resources and equipment. With a tractor, hybrid seed, modern fertilizers, and a reaper, the farmer very sharply increased his yield. In education we are now reaching this kind of transition, and just as the old-fashioned farmers viewed all the new machinery with deep suspicion, many of us wonder what effect new media of instruction will have on teachers.

Insofar as the new media produce results, the effect is bound to be good. In certain schools, teachers now are failing not because they are stupid, untrained, or lazy, but because they are severely overburdened. Like the old-fashioned farmer who hardly had a moment to eat, they need help; and "if, as seems clear, some of the functions performed by human beings can be performed as well or better through other agencies, teachers could assume versatile, differentiated, *human* roles in the schools."[4] Instead of leading students through the lockstep of a single program, they could assist them in the progress of individualized instruction; they could help them discover things for themselves instead of trying to tell them everything; they could draw on local development capital to support programs tailored to specific needs.

In effect, the teacher will become a manager of instruction. Like the school official, he will gain access to a variety of outside services, and operate within a flexibility of form that he has never before enjoyed. Since schools will be able, through performance contracting, to test programs locally before adopting them, teachers will be called on not to initiate untried proposals but rather to take over the operation of programs that are already familiar and successful.

Benefits for School Administrators

In chapter six we argued that educational engineering can ease the problems of desegregation and lower the dropout rate. The solution in each case is the same. If a child can begin to master a skill, no matter what his *pace* of learning, he has both a source of satisfaction or self-respect, and an opportunity, in time, to join his peers in the normal course of instruction. When a student feels hopeless and discouraged, he may leave school; and when he lags far behind his peers, he is more of a drag on the class than a contributor to it. In each case, what he needs is rapid, esteem-building progress in learning basic skills.

Until school officials can assure this kind of progress, their level of authority will continue to decline. Disciplinary problems will become even more common, as will the use of various forms of power to handle them. Please note the sharp distinction between authority and power. Whereas power is derived from simple force, such as the use of police or disciplinary action, authority is de-

---

4. Commission on Instructional Technology, *To Improve Learning* (U.S. Government Printing Office, 1970), page 29.

rived from respect for the moral purposes of an institution. A tyrant, of whatever magnitude, relies on power in this sense; a leader, on his authority. It seems clear that, apart from a certain fringe, our rebellious youth are, in effect, demanding that reliance on power be replaced by responsive authority and that our institutions, including our schools, live up to their promises.

To win respect as educators we need only teach students the necessary skills. Educational engineering is designed to help us do that.

Benefits for All

In particular, what will educational engineering help us do? What are its advantages?

First, it will allow decision makers on every level, from the federal government to the local school board, to govern the system instead of dealing with one crisis after another. They can set firm goals and hold others accountable for results.

Second, it will allow us to halt the waste of dollars on educational failures. When a government experiments and fails, the bureaucracy continues to grow; but when a business fails, it goes out of business and another takes its place. Under educational engineering, if a program does not meet performance criteria, dollars flow back to the federal till, and administrators will know which schools should not receive grants until they make changes.

Third, it will stimulate the creation of a much more advanced technology of instruction. Inflexible and unvalidated instructional materials and techniques such as textbooks and lectures simply aggravate the problems of a group system of teaching and are clearly inadequate for individual instruction. How could such methods possibly provide the feedback that a student needs to improve? Instead, they keep him in a lockstep and expose him to failure.

Fourth, it will allow us to match the talents and resources of private industry to local needs, on local terms, under local control, through the intermediary of management support.

Fifth, it will foster economy by reducing the cost of effective implementation of successful programs, and by highlighting the relatively low cost effectiveness of some programs now widely used.

Sixth, it will give educational personnel an incentive for performance. For example, instructional personnel working under performance contracts can be rewarded on a merit basis, if the school so desires, with bonuses based on learning productivity indexes suitably weighted to match the circumstances.

Seventh, it will give the public sufficient data so that each community can meaningfully assess the governance of the schools, instead of concentrating, as now so often happens, on peripheral issues such as dress codes.

Eighth, it will change the teaching role from mere information-giving to the management of learning. In many classrooms now the only person who is actively and consistently engaged is the teacher. What if every child in that room were as fully absorbed as the teacher? The teacher would not find his job any easier, but he would undoubtedly be more satisfied.

Above all, we will finally have a process through which good educational practice, wherever it is found or developed, can become standard practice in a growing number of schools. Some critics say we lack the necessary educational research; others, that the schools are inept even at running the programs they have. Whatever truth we may find in those charges, the fact remains that our thorniest problem in education lies *between* the research on learning and the routine administration of schools. We have lacked a mechanism for applying much of what we already know. We have isolated examples of good practice all over the country, but we have no sufficient way of standardizing this practice.

The Challenge to Public Education

Educational engineering is linked both to school administration, for which it is a method, and to basic research, on which it depends for knowledge. Its main function, however, is to mediate between the school and the sources of innovation.

In discussing "how to combat the almost inevitable movement of an organization toward elaborateness, rigidity and massiveness and away from simplicity, flexibility and manageable size,"[5] John Gardner, a veteran of the worlds of the university, the foundation, the federal bureaucracy, and the voluntary association, observed that a classic bureaucracy can manage to renew itself in part by calling in a variety of outside servicing organizations. He points out that corporations routinely call on lawyers, auditors, manage-

5. John W. Gardner, *Self-Renewal* (New York: Harper Colophon, 1965), page 80.

ment consultants, and many other specialists who work for a variety of firms in turn. Although their names appear only on contracts, not on the organization chart, few corporations could exist without them. In fact, as Gardner points out:

> The remarkable range of such professional and technical services that are available, plus the flexibility of the contractual relationship, gives the modern organization a wide range of choice in shaping its own future. Within limits, top management can put its finger on almost any function within the organization and decree that henceforth that function will be performed by an outside organization on contract. For the organization that wishes to maintain the maneuverability so essential to renewal, this offers priceless opportunities.[6]

Can we apply this wisdom to public education? The need for renewal in the schools is very clear. It remains for us to take advantage of the opportunities extended by the newly developed process of educational engineering.

6. Gardner, *Self-Renewal*, page 84.

Exhibits

INTRODUCTION TO EXHIBITS

This section presents summaries of and excerpts from the actual documents involved in establishing the program of accountability in Texarkana (Exhibits A through G) and the response of other federal agencies and local school systems to the possibilities and realities of accountability in education (Exhibits H and I).

Background

In the summer of 1969 the U.S. Office of Education announced that funds for dropout prevention programs were available through Title VIII of ESEA. The community of Texarkana, Texas/Arkansas had a serious dropout problem, and submitted a proposal for a program for their community to the Office of Education (Exhibit A). There was already established in Texarkana a viable Model Cities program funded by the Department of Housing and Urban Development (HUD). (The Model Cities program is designed to improve blighted areas to the extent that they can be used as models for other U.S. cities' improvement programs.)

On the basis of the need shown in Exhibit A and the proposed program outlined there, the Office of Education allocated Texarkana $20,000 to retain a management support group—outside assistance—to help them develop their proposal more specifically. Excerpts from the proposal the MSG helped develop are reprinted as Exhibit B.

On the basis of the proposal as outlined in Exhibit B, the Texarkana program was funded and given the go-ahead by the U.S. Office of Education. Exhibit C thus represents one of the first steps in carrying out the formal project—Texarkana's request for bids from outside contractors. Exhibit D is basically an addendum to C; it describes the Rapid Learning Center in more detail.

Exhibit E represents the successful bidder's response—one of ten submitted—to the RFP, and Exhibit F is the formal contract between the successful bidder (Dorsett) and the school district, as approved by the local school board and the Office of Education.

Exhibit G illustrates the special contract negotiated with the independent auditor to assess the results of the program.

Exhibit H represents another recent response of a federal agency to the process of accountability. It is a request from the Department of Health, Education, and Welfare for outside agencies to develop manuals for designing other educational projects in accountability.

Exhibit I is an excerpt from the Dallas, Texas, RFP for developing their accountability project. It illustrates more specifically the duties of the MSG and the auditor with special emphasis on their turnkey provisions.

Although the IEAA has not yet reported on the final results of the Texarkana program as this book goes to press, early test scores encouraged the Office of Economic Opportunity to fund a 5.5 million dollar accountability project for slow learners in eighteen school systems, ranging from large cities to small towns.

Many other exhibits could be included as the idea of accountability continues to gain popularity, but restrictions of space and time confine us to these few as we go to press.

Exhibit A

**Preliminary Dropout Prevention Proposal
from Texarkana to the U.S.
Office of Education**

Preliminary Dropout Prevention Proposal from Texarkana to the U.S. Office of Education [1]

SUMMARY

The purpose of this proposal [submitted on December 13, 1968] is to reduce the number of dropouts of three Texarkana school districts by establishing a contractor-operated "Educational Achievement Center" [called Rapid Learning Center (RLC) elsewhere] for potential dropouts with educational deficiencies, and to establish a Work Study Program for students who might drop out for financial reasons.

The proposal is for a multi-year demonstration and operational program. Specifically, we hope to accomplish the following:

To develop a contractor-operated Educational Achievement Center whose goal will be to eliminate educational deficiencies in reading, math and communication skills.

To develop a Work Study component utilizing the local Chamber of Commerce and local business; the program will provide finances and jobs to students who drop out of school to go to work.

To test and evaluate new methods of creating incentives for teaching; and to establish criteria for measuring the effectiveness of teaching techniques and provide compensation for the level of effectiveness rather than for the number of students passed through the Educational Achievement Center.

Reimbursement to employers for expenses incurred in the Work Study component will be contingent on the student's performance on tests at the end of the term.

Teachers will be trained in the Educational Achievement Center as a part of the program and successful components will be integrated into the regular school curriculum. Management techniques demonstrating cost effectiveness will be utilized.

---

1. Two sections that deal with the "Educational Achievement Center" have been put together in this version.

Evaluation will be built into the project in terms of specifying achievement of students as the basis for payment to the contractor.

Current Dropout Situation in Texarkana Schools

A review of twenty-three studies on the problems of dropouts showed that in twenty of the twenty-three studies, academic difficulties were the primary cause of school dropouts. In nine of these studies, failure and retention in a grade was found to be a major factor in the background of most school dropouts.

The Liberty Eylau School District has conducted a study showing that most students drop out because they are hopelessly behind their peers. A smaller number drop out to earn money "to buy a car," etc.

While the Texarkana, Arkansas, and Texarkana, Texas, School Districts have made no study, counselors report their students drop out for these same reasons.

Model Neighborhood[2] residents account for more than *eighty* percent of all dropouts in Texarkana schools. Because of the lack of resources there have been no programs aimed at dropout prevention. . . .

Rural families migrate to Texarkana to take advantage of low-skilled but high-paying jobs in local defense plants. Their children never enroll in school. A large number of school-age children are employed full-time in local merchandising and restaurant facilities. Other students check out of school, saying they are moving. They never leave Texarkana.

The anticipated dropout rate is much higher than the rate at present. *In the Arkansas School System there is a discrepancy of median percentile achievement of the Iowa Achievement Test [ITBS] of almost 70 points between schools inside the Model Neighborhood and those outside.* In 1969 the Arkansas School System will be integrated and the result will be that students from the Model Neighborhood with the lowest achievement record will be thrown into a new school environment where they must compete with more educationally advantaged classmates.

2. See introduction to Exhibit section.

Model Neighborhood students far behind in achievement standards will find it impossible to compete with their peers.

A similar situation exists in Texarkana, Texas, High School which is in its first semester as a totally integrated facility. All-Negro Dunbar High School was closed in May of 1968. A crisis with deficient students from Dunbar High is expected in the next three academic semesters.

While roughly thirty percent of all students in Texarkana come from families earning less than $2,000 per year, more than seventy percent of all Model Neighborhood students come from families earning less than $2,000 per year.

There is a lack of support personnel in the school systems for deficient students. For example in the Arkansas schools there is one counselor for 1000 students, and one Physical Education teacher per 1100 elementary students. The situation with regard to support personnel in Texarkana, Texas, is one counselor per 1000 students. Liberty Eylau has one counselor for 2800 students.

Teachers in the Arkansas School System will face a new experience working in the integrated high school. The Texas School System will have completed its first academic year with this new experience. The residues of the segregated situation and the problems inherent in going through the desegregation process will drain off the already insufficient administrative, supervisory, and supportive resources.

The failure of many teachers to understand the causes of learning deficiencies and the [small amount] of attention they will be able to spare to students at the bottom of their classes will compound the dropout problem. There will be attitudinal adjustments to be made on the part of [many] of the teaching personnel. They will need support in dealing with the strains and stresses caused by the sudden shift to a new academic environment. Teachers acting as consultants to the [Educational] Achievement Center will be sensitized to this situation.

Educational Achievement Center

Current developments in educational technology permit the use of programmed learning and related methods in a specific and efficient manner.

Educational deficiencies in reading, math and communication skills are a major reason for dropouts and loss of motivation. Upgrading of these skills in grades six through twelve will substantially reduce the number of dropouts.

A separate learning facility operated by an outside contractor is the best place to demonstrate new techniques. Once proved successful, they may be integrated into the regular curriculum.

Efforts to insure reading and math performance in grades one through six will have significant impact on reducing the number of dropouts in grades six through twelve.

Concentrated efforts to induce out-of-school dropouts to enroll in the Educational Achievement Center and eventually to again enroll full-time in school will be demonstrated.

Long-term comprehensive educational planning is necessary if a community is to adequately meet future educational needs.

This proposal is an integral part of projected educational needs and plans for the community as specified in the Texarkana, Arkansas, and Texarkana, Texas, Model Cities One and Five Year Action Plans. This program has direct relationship on future program development in other areas, such as development of vocational training facilities and efforts aimed at raising the overall quality of life of the Model Neighborhood residents.

Community understanding and involvement is essential to the success of the program. Local community organizations and program subcommittees operating in conjunction with the City Demonstration Agency will interpret the program to the Model Neighborhood and the community at large. They will be assisted by a professional team of neighborhood organizers.

Cooperation and coordination of three school districts in two states will be demonstrated.

The school districts will develop a problem-oriented program custom-made for the needs of Texarkana, U.S.A. The school districts will retain total policy and contract control; however, they will coordinate with local groups such as the two City Demonstration Agencies (Model Cities), the Chamber of Commerce, and local business interests.

Major innovations in the proposal are managerial and administrative. The value of the demonstration will be to show

how well and under what conditions the program approach can be made to work.

The effect of the demonstration depends on the scope of inclusion of proven techniques in the curriculum of local and other schools.

It is difficult to conduct demonstration projects in local schools. Texarkana schools lack planning and management personnel. The political and social ramifications of experimentation often limit the use of new approaches. If a school system commits itself to a new approach, political necessity dictates that it must be successful. This inhibits interest in the factors and variables which contribute most or least to any degree of success. Therefore, for demonstration purposes it is desirable to have a separately managed but supplementary remediation center.

One of the most difficult problems in education is to insure "quality control" over the educational process. It is difficult to determine the cost of a student's per-unit instructional achievement. A separately managed center provides a greater opportunity to determine more precisely minimal time, cost and resource requirements for grade-level increases in subject matter like reading and math for students in the Texarkana area.

The separately managed project provides a political buffer for the school. It also provides a highly demonstrable mechanism to get community interest and community support for the concept. Proving techniques before spending local money should be particularly attractive to local taxpayers.

In order to insure effective integration of proven techniques into the school curriculum, school involvement and commitment is essential. In this proposal, the Contractor will hire and train local teachers and para-professionals to act as expert consultants for the Contractor. This will build a cadre of trained teachers in the local school systems.

Moreover, the Contractor will give specifications for nonexpendable capital equipment, and other nonexpendable items; the school districts will purchase such equipment, be reimbursed, and will lease the equipment to the Contractor for the length of the project.

At the end of a particular phase or cycle the school will have trained "teachers," a group of teachers' aides, and non-expendable capital equipment to be used in any program that is integrated into the regular school curriculum.

Specific instructional innovations have not yet been determined. However, this is consistent with our management approach and explicit in the performance specifications which must be met by the Contractors:

The Contractor must agree to be reimbursed on the basis of learning achievements of the students in a designated time period, measured by mutually acceptable testing procedures.

The instructional approach and strategies chosen must be non-teacher or labor intensive. The cost of the program must [either remain] constant or decrease over time and volume.

The media of presentation as well as content must have been proven, and, at a minimum, must have shown high promise in an industrial or university laboratory situation. The innovational purpose is to integrate the various components, media, and trained teachers into a total learning system.

The procedures used by the Contractor for such integration *must* be made available to various school systems as they wish to utilize them in their regular curriculum.

Criteria for choice of the Contractor will be made on the basis of past performance, cost-unit achievement per maximum time period, and uniqueness of method and approach. *We anticipate that several Contractors will be able to guarantee a one grade-level increase in reading and math for no more than $325 and no more than 200 instructional hours per student.*

The phasing of this program will follow the general outline described below:

Phase I (July 1, 1969-September 1970):

A concentrated effort will be made to eliminate learning deficiencies for junior and senior high potential dropouts. A target group of 650 students will be designated. They will require approximately two grade-level increases in at least two subject matter areas. Approximately twenty teachers from the local school districts will participate and approximately fifty para-professionals and teachers' aides will be hired by the Contractor. Concurrent with this operational program, plans for implementing Phase II will have begun.

Phase II (September 1971-July 1974):

Concentrated efforts will be made to provide remedial math and reading in grades one through six for those students designated as potential dropouts or socially disadvantaged. Approximately 750 students [who will require as much as three grade-level increases, especially in reading] will be enrolled part-time in the Center. . . . The cost of instruction will be less because of the age level and because the techniques of instruction will be perfected to a high level of efficiency at this time. Concurrent with the initiation of this phase managerial assistance will be provided to assist the local school to integrate into the junior high and senior high schools' curriculums those techniques proved effective in Phase I. Particular emphasis will be on design and implementation of a scheduling system geared toward individual instruction and an instructional management system which provides school officials with the information regarding student performance, quality control, and cost per student achievement.

The cost of transporting students to the Achievement Facility [Center] will be a necessary program cost.

The school districts will be responsible for the following:

The school districts will contract directly with the Contractor which *they select* based on the criteria mentioned above.

The school districts and the Contractor will develop the criteria for selecting students and will determine the educational deficiencies which need to be corrected. Criteria for accepting the students back into school on a full-time basis will also be determined.

The Achievement Center will use the services of a Project Manager who will be responsible to school districts or their delegated executive agents to insure that the Contractor will fulfill his contract agreements.

The school districts will coordinate the planning and development of this program with a long-range educational goal for the community. This plan is an integral part of a coordinated attack of problems affecting the quality of life in Texarkana, U.S.A. This attack is spelled out in the Texarkana, Arkansas, and the Texarkana, Texas Model Cities Action Plans.

The commitment to the schools and to the program of local groups such as the Texarkana Chamber of Commerce will be utilized to gain the cooperation and participation of the business community.

The commitment of Model Cities Program subcommittees and neighborhood organizations along with the Model Cities community newspaper, the *Developer*, will be used to secure broad-based community support for the schools and for the program.

Management

An essential element in the success of the program will be the project management support provided to the schools. Specifically, assistance will be provided in: program proposals and development, preparation of requests for proposals, negotiations and Contractor selection, [and] management planning for implementation and research.

[The preliminary proposal also discusses a "Work Study Program" for potential dropouts and the relation of other community plans to the Education Achievement Center and the Work Study Program.]

Exhibit B

**Excerpts from Texarkana's
Formal Project Application to
the U.S. Office of Education**

EXCERPTS FROM TEXARKANA'S FORMAL PROJECT APPLICATION TO THE U.S. OFFICE OF EDUCATION

[Sections I and II are omitted.]

III. PROGRAM PLANNING

Introduction:

Program planning and evaluation have to be a continuing process, especially in a program which has both operational and experimental components. Moreover, planning has to include the early involvement of all parties who will conceivably participate if the NIH (not-invented-here) factor is to be minimized. This is particularly true in a program where an outside group (e.g., the contractor which will operate the RLC [Rapid Learning Center]) will be demonstrating techniques which, upon being proven effective, will be integrated into the school's instructional programs and general environment. At the same time, in order to actually implement instructional program improvements throughout the entire school system, which is one of the underlying objectives, those political and social forces outside of the school system must also be aware of what is going on in such a way that they can readily perceive their vested interests (e.g., taxpayer or citizen associations are presented specific information on potential cost savings). In short, to plan an operational program which is experimental and also is conducted in a political and social environment, one necessarily has to put politics into planning.

Planning Design:

The conceptual approach taken in this project evolved out of discussions in December, 1968 between Charles Blaschke, Manager, Education Programs, and Dr. Joseph Hart, Staff Consultant, Institute for Politics and Planning, the three school superintendents, and other interested parties. Based on a discussion of the conceptual approach and its apparent feasibility in solving local dropout problems, the School Districts jointly drafted and submitted a preliminary proposal to USOE and were notified in February 1969 that they had been selected as a potential grantee. A planning grant was authorized in March and the school systems asked the Institute for Politics and Planning to provide assistance in planning operational programs. The contract between the Fiscal Agent and the Institute was effected. Performance of work began March 13th with preliminary action having been taken prior to that time.

Study and Analysis:

Implicit in the management plan . . . is a methodology based on the above philosophy.

Data on the nature and extent of the dropout problem in Texarkana, U.S.A., schools were gathered from the following sources:

A. Standardized and national achievement test results (ITBS [Iowa Test of Basic Skills] and the SRA [Science Research Associates' Achievement Series]).

B. Existing studies attempting to determine the reason for students' dropping out, interviews with teachers, counselors, tutors, and potential as well as recent dropouts, Model City surveys, and other data sources were gathered and analyzed.

A review was made of several hundred projects which related directly or indirectly to the dropout proposal. The staff then analyzed 25 which were most relevant and germane to particular problems. National assessment studies as well as the most recent analyses of dropout prevention programs conducted by the federal government, especially USOE and its contractors, were carefully studied and analyzed to determine the factors which would be included in experimental objectives as well as the feasibility of approaches to be used in the operational program.

Community and Participants' Involvement:

The community at large became aware of the potential project beginning as early as January, 1969, [when] the goals and objectives and, most importantly, unique approaches taken were described in detail. At least six newspaper editorials and news items appeared over the next four months. State newspapers also printed several notices of the planning grant award and a description of the project.

Discussions were held with individuals who had worked and/or presently are working on related projects.

The following groups were briefed in detail, suggestions from them were sought, and substantive areas in which operational relationships would exist were agreed upon:

A. Chamber of Commerce—Work Study Program: solicit industry support, approve OJT [on-the-job training] reimbursement procedures. (Phase II)

B. Ten churches—RLC: assist in recruiting professionals for contractor, data gathering on dropout problem.

C. Both City Halls—Availability of their facilities for planning and data gathering. Model City CDAs [City Demonstration Agencies] were especially helpful in providing data.

D. Police Chiefs—Data on relationship between dropouts and juvenile delinquency problem.

State/Federal Agencies Contacted:

No operational plan can expect support from the funding agency without a reiterative relationship — including feedback on objectives as well as procedures — regarding the project. In order to expedite development of a proposal which would meet stated and unstated guidelines of federal or state approving agencies, the following agencies were contacted and briefed on the details of the project. Suggestions and comments were incorporated into various drafts.

    A. Texas and Arkansas Department of Education [were contacted] through personal visits by IPP [Institute of Politics and Planning] staff and telephone calls requesting recommendations and suggestions. (Three meetings, Arkansas and two meetings, Texas)

    B. Program officers as well as commissioners at the USOE [U.S. Office of Education] a total of seven separate visits involving over 25 people. USOE program monitor and IPP staff have met on four occasions.

    C. Representatives from twelve interested state departments in Arkansas were briefed on the Dropout Prevention Program by local and IPP staff members.

    D. Letters and phone calls regarding progress and intent were sent and made to various state departments in Texas during the duration of the program. Regional (USOE and TEA [Texas Education Agency]) officials were also informed in a similar manner.

Legislators and Representatives Contacted:

Because this project has implications beyond the limits of the school systems in Texarkana, it was necessary and felt appropriate to contact political leaders and representatives who should be made aware of the project and its implications. With this purpose in mind, the following officials were contacted:

    A. Arkansas state representatives, including the state senator, who is a local school board member and the president of the Arkansas State School Board Association, and the Speaker of the House.

    B. Congressmen from each of the two districts and three of the four senators of the two states and/or appropriate staff members.

    C. Additional congressmen including all but one of the Arkansas delegation, plus two congressmen from the Texas delegation (other than those mentioned above). They were briefed on the significance and implications of this particular project.

Other groups which have been contacted and/or have been sent information, or have contacted school officials or IPP staff members include:

    A. National Education Association (Division of Research)

    B. American Council on Education

C. Six other schools (LEAs) applying for similar program grants
D. Numerous individuals and two journals in the area of education technology and innovation
E. At least 15 corporations which would be considered potential contractors have been alerted to the ensuing RFP.

Teacher, School Personnel, and Student Involvement:

Selected teachers/counselors submitted evaluation papers describing the local dropout situation. Staff members conducted followup interviews.

School officials, Model City CDA officials, teachers, and other interested parties were contacted and briefed along with other community groups who had vested interests or would be affected by the program. While the specific tasks and groups are listed or are implicit in the Management Plan, the following groups were briefed in detail:

A. Youth Organizations and Neighborhood Youth Councils – Work-Study: operational participation as well as general policies to be followed.
B. Civic Clubs – RLC and Work-Study: general support.
C. Classroom Teachers Association – (Liberty-Eylau and Texarkana, Arkansas) RLC: recommendations of teachers to participate: suggestion [of] future teachers' workshops based on RLC. . . .

Creation of Program Development Advisory Committee:

In order to insure an intimate, genuine working relationship between the IPP staff and the various groups of school officials whose knowledge and support of the program will be responsible for its long-run success, a Program Development Advisory Committee was created during the planning period. The Committee consisted of three counselors, three teachers, three school board members, the three school superintendents, and three staff members familiar with federal programs.

The purpose of the PDAC, its membership, and minutes can be made available upon request. In short, it was a working group which advised the IPP staff and the other parties involved in developing the final draft proposal regarding the nature and extent of the dropout problem, the causes, and the feasibility of various solutions. It also provided liaison with the representative groups in the schools.

In retrospect, the major contribution of this group was:

A. Penetrating analyses of the causes of the dropouts beyond those indicated by general statistics.
B. Indications of receptivity on the part of various schools, students, and other groups to the dropout prevention project.
C. Suggestions regarding the relationship of this project to the other on-going or planned projects.

D. Specific program proposals which should be initiated in Phases II
and III to prevent dropouts at earlier grade levels and due to reasons other than academic achievement.

Final Action:

Copies of the draft proposal were submitted to the three school superintendents on April 23. The Arkansas board was briefed individually
prior to the general meeting on April 28, attended also by members of
the two state departments of education and the USOE program monitor.
After a four-hour discussion, unanimous approval was made. The
Liberty-Eylau and the Texarkana, Arkansas, school board had authorized the two superintendents that perogative which was exercised the
following day. Two major points were emphasized upon approval: (a)
that local control based on the proposal would be exercised; and (b)
that if the decision of the Texas Independent School District Board to
submit a "Freedom of Choice" plan resulted in its losing federal support,
the other two participating schools in compliance (Liberty-Eylau and
Arkansas) [could] and would continue to participate in the project. . . .

IV. OBJECTIVES

[Although this Formal Project Application was originally submitted to
the U.S. Office of Education on May 3, 1969, long before the contractor
was chosen, it was revised on March 5, 1970, and thus includes information on Dorsett, as follows:]

The Rapid Learning Center Managers (professionals) will utilize
effectively the new techniques for individualized instruction concentrating on the Dorsett M86 Audio-Visual Teaching Machine and its programs, but also utilizing other programmed materials. Effectiveness will
be determined on the basis of student attendance in the Rapid Learning
Center and a rating scale to be administered by the Internal Evaluators
and the Project Manager.

The paraprofessionals will demonstrate an ability to assist Rapid
Learning Center students in operating the equipment and becoming
familiar with the IBM Card Port-a-Punch System and keep up-to-date
records on all the Rapid Learning Center activities. These activities will
be measured by a student questionnaire and a checklist developed by
the Dorsett Resident Director with the aid of the Project Director.

One hundred and fifty students will be enrolled in the Rapid Learning
Centers to receive individualized instruction in reading. Students were
selected by the counselors, volunteered for the program or were randomly selected from [those who scored at] the lower 25th percentile of
the Iowa Test of Basic Skills and Science Research Associates' Achieve-

ment Test. The typical student has an IQ of 75 or over and will be two or more grade levels behind in reading. As a result of eighty hours of instruction in the Rapid Learning Center these students will be raised one grade level in reading, measured by the Iowa Test of Basic Skills and Science Research Associates' [Achievement] Test.

One hundred and fifty students will be enrolled in the Rapid Learning Centers to receive individualized instruction in math. Students were selected by the counselors, volunteered for the program, or were randomly selected from [those who scored at] the lower 25th percentile of the Iowa Test of Basic Skills and Science Research Associates' Achievement Test. The typical student has an IQ of 75 or over and will be two or more grade levels behind in math. As a result of eighty hours of instruction in the Rapid Learning Center these students will be raised one grade level in math, measured by the Iowa Test of Basic Skills and Science Research Associates' [Achievement] Test.

Parents of project students will support the project as determined by their attendance at several meetings with project staff during the year to discuss their children's progress or difficulties and by their volunteering and working in the Rapid Learning Center in an effort to become more familiar with the program. In turn parent advisory groups [will] be formed to facilitate dissemination [of information] and gain greater support for the program among residents of the target community. Measurement of parental response will be based on records kept by the project staff, and a questionnaire distributed among the parents.

The Project Director will display knowledge of effective management procedures as indicated by the production of a printed manual on operational policies and monitoring feedback, supplied by the Internal Evaluator and evaluated by the Outside Educational Auditor and the Internal Evaluators, . . . [to assure] that policies were followed at least ninety percent of the time.

The Dorsett Educational Systems, Inc. will operate the six Rapid Learning Centers to prevent dropouts. An attempt will be made to erase the academic deficiencies of students in grades seven through twelve (7-12) in math and reading. They will also assist in the in-service training of the Texarkana teachers in order for the successful components of the Rapid Learning Center [to] be implemented into the existing Texarkana curriculum. A checklist to evaluate all materials used is being made available to all teachers. Dorsett will be paid eighty dollars ($80) per eighty (80) hours of instruction, guaranteeing one grade-level [increase] in math and reading.

The Texarkana, U.S.A., school administration will support the Rapid Learning Center concept and will implement the successful portions of the Rapid Learning Center program in the existing regular school classrooms. The school administration will also contribute to the Title VIII program, personnel, equipment, and materials. The measurement instrument will be a checklist provided by the Internal Evaluator and filled out by teachers, principals, and supervisors in the Texarkana system.

V. PROGRAM PROCEDURES

General Objective:

Over a five-year period (Phase I-V), improve the quality of the Texarkana Schools' instructional programs for students who would normally drop out for academic reasons.

Specific Objectives:

In Phase I, Dorsett Educational Systems, Inc. is operating six RLCs for potential dropouts in grades 7-12. These students are being instructed to achieve satisfactory gains in reading and math. At the same time research will be directed at the nature and extent of the dropout problem in Texarkana. The Centers [will] also provide the opportunity for determining the demonstration value of experimental approaches and for maximizing the demonstration effect for replication purposes, locally and otherwise. Also, through participation of parents in the RLC and their spreading information about the RLC program, attitudinal changes will be brought about within the target area families. The performance objectives of this component are operation, research and development, and demonstration.

1. *Operation Objectives*
   A. To increase the levels of academic achievement of 150–400 potential dropouts by two grade levels in math and reading in grades 7-12, on a guaranteed performance basis. On this basis the contractor is accountable for the learning of each student in the RLC. Ninety percent of the potential dropouts should remain in school rather than drop out after [completing] the program and [reentering] . . . school full time.

   The most objective evaluative measurement will be based on terms of increased achievement and cost per unit of achievement.

   [B]. To remove deficiencies in study and communications skills so that students can reenter school full time with low probability of dropping out. Based on interviews with teachers, counselors, and potential participants and youth tutors, it is felt that there will be a need to provide corrective as well as instructional measures in these areas for over half of the participants. This projection is further substantiated by the find that the students in Washington Junior High School at the 9th grade were fifty-four percentile points lower than those [in the] 9th grades at Jefferson Avenue Junior High School in study skills. Individual programs will be "tailored" according to individual needs.

Continuous research and analysis [will] be done to accurately predict the probability of homogeneous groups of students in grades 7-12; and to project the nature and extent of the educational and directly related deficiencies inherent in existing school programs.

[C]. To train thirty teachers who will be working as "consultants" for the contractor.

Although the contractor will hire the instructional staff, both professional and paraprofessional "aides," the school system teachers will work closely with the contractor in order to become familiar with and capable of utilizing the instructional techniques and materials in their classrooms. Phase II, by the contractor and school consultant, will modify the instructional curriculum where needed and hold [a] limited number of in-service training sessions for other teachers.

Visible curriculum changes during Phase II will systematically measure the integration of instructional methods and materials into the school system and the effective use of a school consultant.

2. *Research and Development*

A. To determine the specific costs and instructional time required for grade levels of achievement of groups of students with similar learning characteristics and profiles. This model will be used by the local school and the Project Manager in planning for Phase II operations as well as integrating economical and effective curricula into the local schools. It will also provide the basis for similar schools to adopt the contractor-operated approach for instructional reform in their particular school.

B. To research and analyze the relationship between educational and directly related deficiencies in K-6 and the probability of the student dropping out at the Junior High and above levels. Hypotheses and a tentative model will be developed which will:

1. Allow for early detection of potential dropouts;
2. Provide insight into the specific factors which contribute directly to low education achievement; and
3. Provide the basis for student selection criteria, determining the nature and extent of the deficiency and indicating the instructional approaches to be developed and tested in Phase II.

C. To develop manuals and multi-media presentations of procedures to be followed by other schools in similar situations in order to adopt the approach taken in Phase I. This will include:

1. Staffing patterns with minimum requirements;
2. Methodologies for analyzing the dropout problem;
3. Development of the RFP;
4. Contractor selection and negotiating procedures;

5. Procedures for determining requirements for program planning and project management assistance to be used by the would-be adopter;

6. Procedures for pinpointing the administrative and managerial problems and feasible solutions which will allow the school actually to realize the potential cost savings and/or performance increases when the most efficient instructional programs tested in the Center are implemented into the operational classrooms in grades 7-12.

3. *Demonstration Objectives*

A. To demonstrate to the local community, school officials, teachers, board members, and appropriate state and federal officials that the educational process, in part if not in whole, is capable of being managed, and specifically:

1. That quality control in math and reading can be introduced at a ninety percent accuracy level of prediction;

2. That diagnostic tests and institutional approaches based on behavioral psychology and educational technology do allow for predictability of student achievement per maximum time period for students with different learning characteristics;

3. That criteria for measuring student achievement in math and reading exist and can be used effectively and objectively;

4. Providing a "credible" experiment whose results and approach have greatest likelihood of being adopted by the schools across the country.

C. To demonstrate to state and federal officials that the contractor-operated approach is the most effective and least disruptive means for:

1. Integrating school systems where large educational achievement differences exist between Negro and other minority-group youth and [their] white counterparts by national standardized tests;

2. Acclimating and training compensatory education and upgrading for those who need it;

3. Providing true and compensatory education and upgrading for those who need it; and

4. Gaining local political and community support for program effectiveness and educational improvement.

D. To document and analyze all the means utilized in initial planning and start-up for getting support of the local community parents, youth groups, and other groups involved in Phase I. A report . . . for the school officials and the layman will be written to supplement a video-tape of the overall program for purposes of state and national [information] dissemination.

GUIDELINES FOR PROPOSAL EVALUATION

Since the time swiftly approaches for the submission of proposals by the contractors who have communicated firm intentions to bid, it is in our interest to draw up guidelines for the evaluation of these proposals. As stated in the RFP, the criteria for selection of a contractor will include:

    a. Soundness of approach
    b. Most favorable pricing arrangement
    c. Past performance and technical ability
    d. Organizational commitment to the approach and goals of the over-
       all project
    e. Other factors

As vague as these criteria are, they form the parameters within which contractor selection takes place. The problem now, before the avalanche of proposals occurs, is to refine the selection criteria so that they are reasonably operational.

Before launching into an explication of the criteria item by item, we need to determine the types of consultants we need to take on for two or three days to evaluate certain proposals. I[1] forecast that we will need the help of experts in the areas of computer assisted instruction, behavioral psychology, and testing. We may be able to find one man who can serve as an expert consultant in both psychology and testing since the two fields are so closely related. Without committing ourselves, we will line up consultants on a tentative and contingent basis. Suggested names should be listed ASAP.

Soundness of Approach:

Of all the criteria soundness of approach is the most general and most difficult to operationalize. Soundness is directly related to the projected feasibility of both the instructional program and the transfer of innovation from RLC to school system. Thus we must evaluate "soundness" in its two aspects, the technical and the technical-socio-political.

In the first phase of the project, the technical function of the contractor is most critical. Although many of the potential contractors will be coming in with some totally new material and techniques, we can be fairly certain that these contractors will offer rationales based on some sort of empirical evidence. If hard data as justification is not present in the proposal (or readily available to us) we should be suspect of the approach proposed. Although this project is meant to be innovative, we don't want it to become experimental at the expense of the school systems involved. Most of the material and techniques proposed will have been field tested and/or based on established principles of behavioral

---

1. A member of the management support group

psychology. Therefore, the expert guidance of a psychologist (or our own knowledge of stimulus/response theory) and a hard look at field-tested material are necessary conditions for evaluating the technical soundness of the approaches proposed.

In the second phase of the program the critical factors are going to be technical and socio-political. Successful transfer of instruction from RLC to regular school procedure depends on the understanding and acceptance of the program by the community at large and particularly those within the school systems involved. This means that "soundness of approach" is, in a very important sense, a matter of what the local community will allow. Thus, each proposal must be evaluated in terms of how well its approach contributes to an equitable balance in the competition for the scarce resources we refer to as "power." Technical aspects are also significant considerations here (e.g., do time and dollars allow for the necessary training of teachers in Phase II?).

Aside from the general comments which I have made concerning "soundness of approach" I would like to add that we should give specific consideration to such factors as:

1. Degree of labor intensiveness
2. Extent to which instruction is individualized
3. Testing instruments proposed and accompanying rationale
4. Plan for training local personnel, both consultants and para-professionals
5. Motivational techniques proposed
6. Management and logistical plan
7. Provisions for quality control and on-going evaluation
8. Range and flexibility of instructional time per day
9. Difficulty of transition of mid-year student transfer from RLC to school system

Most Favorable Pricing Arrangement:

In determining the most favorable pricing arrangement we need to develop an accounting system that will allow us to reduce to common denominators the various components of the project, in spite of the fact that the contractors will be proposing different methods of cost reimbursement. Generally costs will fall into three categories (1) start-up, (2) capital [outlay], and (3) operating.

(1) *Start-up costs* include all extraordinary, one-time expenditures, with the exception of capital outlay. Perhaps the major start-up cost will be the training of paraprofessionals. In most cases the proposals will have these costs computed into operating expenses. If it isn't apparent what the start-up costs are, then we ask the contractor for his estimates.

(2) The two most significant items of *capital outlay* will be the re-

furbishing of the RLC and the purchase of instructional hardware. Special criteria for evaluating equipment are discussed later in this report.

(3) *Operating costs* are all those expenses incurred in the normal operation of the RLC. In accounting these costs, which are in fact the most significant since they relate most directly to Phase II, we must come up with a system that is not only informative but also easy to work with. The accounting system worked out in the management SOP [standard operating procedure] is probably adequate for the proposal evaluation and need not be duplicated here.

An effective accounting system is only one side of the coin in making a rational evaluation of the proposed pricing arrangements. A significant variable in determining cost per unit achievement is the learning capability and potential of each student. We assume that each student selected to participate in the program is capable of attaining [his appropriate] grade level. Nevertheless, [the] rate of progress toward this goal will vary from student to student. . . .

Past Performance and Technical Ability

The process of judging past performance and technical ability involves gathering together as much relevant information as possible regarding the previous projects and "production" of each contractor. For obvious reasons we cannot rely merely on information provided by the contractor in his proposal. Thus a good deal of reconnaissance work has been done and will continue to be done by the IPP [Institute of Politics and Planning] staff.

Technical ability is a potential that is, in part, verified by actual performance. In turn, performance is something done, something that can be reported as an event and measured. There is a difference between spending ten years thinking about building a better mousetrap and the act of actually building it. We must keep this difference in mind.

All the contractors will be coming in with some sort of past performance. The question that remains is the degree to which this performance is relevant to the present project. Relevant activities include the research and development of instructional hardware and software materials, offering instruction on a guaranteed performance basis, instructional work with children from low income families, experience with contingency management, and the operation of job corps centers. Once we get a good picture of what the contractor has done, we are in a good position to evaluate his record. This involves contacting and questioning the previous consumers of the contractor's production.

Another component of past performance is related to the experience of the contractor's personnel. Each of the proposals should list personnel who have been engaged in activities similar to those listed in the previous paragraph. Furthermore, we should be on the lookout for people who evidence some degree of management expertise, especially when new consortia are being created for this project. Although it is not necessary to play up the importance of academic credentialization, I think it is essential to see evidence of people who have had formal training in the social and behavioral sciences and "real world" education.

Organizational Commitment

Perhaps the single most important factor in determining organizational commitment is indicated by the calibre of personnel which the contractor is willing to involve in the project, and the verbal and other indications of commitment from high-level corporate executives. Within the contractor's organization, evidence of high-level management support is absolutely essential. The contractor's investment of time and other resources in planning the proposal is another important factor here.

We must be wary of those who come in with pre-packaged system designs. The pre-packaged design is an indication that one is peddling a solution without careful consideration of the stated problems. Super-salesmen who preach their approach as a panacea to all problems are suspect. Although we can assume that the contractor is motivated in part by the possibility of making a profit we should see some indication of a strong desire to establish a favorable "track record" of successful performance, thus looking at this project as a market-creating device for long-run profit.

Since this project represents challenges that exceed the capability of any existing organization, we should look favorably on newly formed consortia arrangements. If consortia are formed we must be sure that they are based on a relationship that will remain viable throughout the duration of the project. This means that we must have an indication of lines of responsibility that will show who within the consortium will handle which specific aspects of the program. Effective management techniques are critical here.

Another aspect of organizational commitment is related to the extent of "other operations" which the contractor is willing to and able to perform. Specifically, we should see what sort of related activities are suggested in each proposal. These related activities (which might be thought as "necessary bonuses") include such things as social services, instructional services for those other than potential dropouts (e.g., mental retardees, adults, and "upward bound" types), and counselling and guidance services.

Other Factors

One of the few constraints listed in the RFP is that the approach used by the contractor be relatively non-labor intensive. This means that one of the most significant components of the program will be related to hardware technology. In evaluating the equipment proposed we should keep in mind the following criteria:

1. Cost effectiveness
2. Availability through GSA "surplus" programs
3. Delivery time
4. Maintenance, re-installation, and amortization costs
5. Flexibility in accepting different kinds of curricular material
6. Adaptability to classroom environments

Obviously the past record of each piece of equipment proposed will be scrutinized carefully in order to ascertain how well it lives up to the claims of the manufacturer. One final caveat regarding equipment: a car that breaks down all the time won't get you where you want to go. Even if the manufacturer has an attractive service contract and agrees to fix the machine for nothing, the down time costs the owner money. . . .

Contract Negotiations

It is highly doubtful that a contractor will be selected purely on the basis of the proposals submitted. Rather there will have to be a round of negotiations with three or four of the best proposals re-submitted. During this negotiation phase each contractor will be wanting more definitive answers in several areas. Most of these questions will be related to standard operating procedure in such areas as testing, transportation, program planning for Phase II, and reporting between the project management office and the contractor's office. In negotiating these questions the management SOP should serve as a guide.

[Sections VI-VIII, which deal with such matters as "Personnel" and "Facilities, Materials, and Equipment," are omitted.]

IX. CONTRACTING

Listed below are the services with the proposed project which are to be subcontracted:

Dorsett Educational Systems, Inc. ....Contractor
EPIC Evaluation ....Outside Educational Auditor
Education Service Center ....Internal Evaluation
C. J. Blaschke ....Management Support Group
All of the above are on a cost reimbursement type of contract.
Funds to be paid under the contract:
Dorsett Educational Systems, Inc. $120,000.00
EPIC Evaluation 5,200.00
Education Service Center 11,500.00
C. J. Blaschke 20,000.00

The general scope of work assumed by Dorsett Educational Systems, Inc. is to organize and operate the instructional component of the first phase of the Texarkana Dropout Prevention Program, to provide instruction in basic reading, math, and study skills to a minimum of two hundred students. The study skills may be measured by inference of the achievement in math and reading areas. [Dorsett is also] to hire and train local personnel. If possible, these people will come from the target area, as paraprofessionals in the operation of the instructional program. [Dorsett will] . . . utilize at least 20 teachers and administrators from the participating school systems who will work part-time in the instructional program and will facilitate the contemplated transfer of the Dorsett material to the Texarkana Rapid Learning Centers. Their first-hand knowledge of the nature and extent of academic problems unique to the Texarkana schools will be useful to the contractor . . . [Dorsett will] . . . operate centers at locations mutually agreeable to the parties.

The purpose of an independent educational accomplishment audit is to establish the facts relative to the status of a project's performance at the time of the audit. The starting point for the audit review will be the statements of project purposes and procedures in the funded proposal. Judgments by the auditors will be confined to the question of whether the project is in fact operating according to prestated objectives, schedules, and procedures. This requirement does not, however, rule out comments or conclusions by the auditor regarding the progress of the project operation at the time of each audit review.

In brief, an educational audit is a check to see whether the LEA did what it proposed to do at specified time periods. The audit reports something that can be seen, recorded, captured, counted, or measured in some way. The educational audit must result in a report. This report may include commendations and recommendations for correcting revealed weaknesses in succeeding phases of the project. It must be locally sponsored and it must be an audit of *local* objectives. It should be made available. It will be made available to the public for its information.

EPIC Evaluation will prepare reports on the status of the project to the LEA, which will forward copies to OE [the Office of Education] at announced dates in order to facilitate decision-making such as continuation actions, amendments, and terminations. A final report on the project will also be prepared for the LEA and OE within three months of the project's termination.

The overall goal of the internal evaluator, Education Service Center, is to provide the project director with information that is needed to make appropriate decisions in the operation and improvement of the program. To provide this information for the Texarkana Dropout Prevention Program, the internal evaluator plans to follow a series of systematic procedures. These procedures will be correlated with and include the necessary steps to cover the provisions contained in the subcontract between the local education agency and Dorsett Educational Systems, Inc.

The internal evaluator will perform the following tasks:
1. Identify and describe the variables involved in the Texarkana Dropout Prevention Program. This will include a description of the people, procedures, programs, and desired behaviors involved in the project.
2. Program objectives will be written by the internal evaluator. These objectives will be written in behavioral terms so that the intended outcomes can be identified and measured.
3. An evaluation design for the project will be developed. This evaluation design will indicate the population involved; and it will outline how each objective will be measured, the type of data to be gathered, when the data will be gathered, and the procedures for analyzing the data.
4. A format for monitoring the program will be developed. This format will be designed to check to see if the proposed program is being implemented as planned and to provide process evaluation information.

The internal evaluator will have frequent contacts with the project in carrying out the above listed tasks. He will work closely with the project director and under his jurisdiction. At the end of the project period, a written evaluation report will be submitted.

Mr. C. J. Blaschke, Manager of Education Programs, Institute of Politics and Planning, served on the Management Support Group. The general scope of work is listed below:
(a) Analyze and determine the nature and extent of the "dropout" problem of the public school districts which will participate, hereinafter described as the "Participants," in the planned dropout prevention project.
(b) Assist the Participants to define and refine to operational terms the overall objectives of the contractor-operated achievement center and work-study program, as indicated in the Preliminary Proposal submitted to USOE on December 16, 1968, hereinafter described as the "Preliminary Proposal."
(c) Assist the Participants to determine the criteria for selecting students who will participate and determine the criteria for measuring the success of the program.
(d) Assist the Participants to convert the objectives of the dropout prevention program to performance specifications and draft a mutually acceptable "request for proposals" which will be sent to potential contractors, after notification of award.
(e) Assist the Participants to develop mutually acceptable criteria for evaluating subcontractor proposals.
(f) Develop and draft for approval an overall operational program plan incorporating all the above and other requirements stipulated in USOE guidelines, as appropriate.

   (g) Develop and present to Participants for consideration of approval an overall multi-year management plan which will include program budgets, costs and schedules, requirements for phasing in and out program elements, and requirements for project management assistance.

   (h) Assist the Participants to develop an overall research and experimental design component.

   (i) Assist the Participants [to] garner local, community, and other support for the effective implementation of the overall project.

   (j) Draft a mutually acceptable final proposal to be submitted to USOE.

There are certain responsibilities retained by the LEA for the control and supervision of the subcontracted services:

   (a) All subcontractors must adhere to all policies and rules as stated in the Texarkana, Arkansas, School District #7, General Bulletin.

   (b) All personnel must be approved by the LEA.

   (c) The Project Director has the responsibility of monitoring progress in all operations and [seeing] that they are being operated within the confines of their subcontractual proposal. . . .

Exhibit C

Request for Proposal That Texarkana
Sent to Prospective Bidders

REQUEST FOR PROPOSAL THAT TEXARKANA
SENT TO PROSPECTIVE BIDDERS

STATEMENT OF WORK

1. *General Conditions*

Only those contractors which meet the following general conditions will be considered potential contractors to operate the Accelerated Learning Achievement Center [ALAC]:

(a) The contractor is willing to be reimbursed for costs of math and reading instruction on the basis of student achievement per maximum periods of instructional time with heavy penalties for failure to meet performance requirements.

(b) The instructional process has to be relatively non-labor (i.e., non-teacher) intensive, [so] that the operating costs per unit of achievement of expanding the operations or of increasing the volume of students participating in the ALAC will decrease over time and as center operations are integrated into school systems. Instruction will be individualized and self-pacing to the greatest extent possible.

(c) The instructional process tested, validated, and demonstrated in the operations of the ALAC can be implemented into the counterpart grade levels within the local school systems without creating unnecessary political and social problems within the community. All personnel and instructional materials will be rec ommended by the Executive Committee [of the project] and approved by the school boards. The contractor will be required to make available such data, procedures, and assistance to the Project Manager or his delegated representatives to facilitate this implementation.

(d) The contractor must demonstrate the general capacity to provide the instruction in study skills development as well as that instruction required to be performed in the conduct of those ancillary programs described [below in section 9, "Related And Ancillary Programs"].

2. *Performance Requirements:*

The overall long-run objective of the Texarkana Dropout Prevention Project is to prevent students from dropping out of school.

The specific objective of this sub-component during this phase of operations is to remove the math, reading, and communications and study skills deficiencies of 150-400 students who will be enrolled in local schools at the 7th through the 12th grade, but will receive accelerated learning for 3-4 hours per day at the ALAC(s). The typical participant selected will be two to three grade levels deficient at the 9th grade level in math and/or reading and will have similar deficiencies in study skills based on [performance on the] Iowa Tests of Basic Skills. Student learning characteristics are described [below in section 11, "Target Population"]. The contractor will be required to remove these deficiencies within an agreed maximum number of hours of instruction.

3. *Methods of Measuring Learning Achievement*

(a) Math and reading. Pre- and post-tests will be utilized as the basis for determining student achievement. Preferred tests to be utilized will be Iowa Tests for Educational Development (ITED). This test has been administered locally several years by the participating schools. However, the contractor might wish to propose another testing instrument or combination (e.g., at different grade levels), in which case a rationale and justification for doing so should be made explicit. In the event that the ITED is used, or if another test or combination is proposed, the proposal should indicate which sub-components of the tests (e.g., reading, natural science, math comprehension, etc.) constitute the "reading" and "math" on which achievement will be based. The Project Manager will reserve the right to test a sample number of the participants at any time after the enrollee has received 20 hours of instruction, and up to three to six months after completion of ALAC instruction to determine actual retention both of which might be the basis of contract re-negotiation. All of the above tests will be administered under the direct supervision of the Project Manager or a specifically delegated group [such as an independent educational accomplishment auditor].

4. *Method of Cost Reimbursement*

In order to achieve the overall objectives, incentives will be allowed for the contractor to [help] the student achieve designated performance levels in the most efficient manner. In proposing the method of reimbursement in response, the contractor might

Exhibit C 177

want to consider one or a combination of the following methods as the basis of his determination:

(a) Fixed fee on a grade-level achievement basis in math and/or reading per maximum hours of instruction on an "all or nothing" basis. (E.g., one grade level in math and reading for $250 in not more than 200 instructional hours. If the student does not achieve at the prescribed levels, then the contractor is not reimbursed the fee.)

(b) Fixed fee based on a grade-level achievement basis in math and reading per maximum hours of instruction or achievement normalized to the maximum hours of instruction with penalty clauses (e.g., if the student achieves only 0.8 grade-level increase in 120 hours, when 100 is the maximum stipulated time, . . . with a penalty clause of 60% between .5 and .7 grade levels of achievement, the contractor would be paid 40% of the stipulated fixed fee.)

(c) Fixed fee basis per "cluster" of study skills with maximum hours not more than one-third of total hours of instruction in math or reading. Behavioral objectives and pre- and post-tests to be used will be stated explicitly.

The bidder may choose to propose an approach other than those above. Such approaches will not be considered when submitted alone but are encouraged when submitted as supplemental to the basic response to this RFP. In the supplemental proposal for cost reimbursement, the rationale and justification must be made quite explicit.

5. *Specific Provisions*

In the proposal, the contractor will agree to the following specific provisions or stipulate reasons to the contrary, and provide descriptive information as described below:

(a) The contractor agrees to hire and train local personnel, most of whom are to be used as paraprofessionals in the ALAC operations. Minimal qualifications will be stipulated for each job slot which would be filled by same. At least 50% of personnel involved in the instructional program will be made by the school board on recommendation of the Executive Committee.

(b) The contractor agrees to utilize approximately 20 teachers and administrators from the participating school, chosen by the Executive Committee as "consultants" who will work part-time at

the ALAC and will be involved in overall design, curricula re-
design and modification, instructional systems development, instruction evaluation, and other areas in which their first-hand
knowledge of the nature and extent of academic problems unique
to the Texarkana schools will be useful to the contractor. The
contractor will be reimbursed for the costs of hiring these consultants — approximately $10,000. Specific areas in which these
local consultants could be used part-time should be stipulated.

(c) The contractor agrees to submit in his proposal a list and
specifications of all non-expendable equipment, materials, as well
as consumable instructional material which will be used in the
ALAC(s). Suggested equipment sales representatives and addresses
should be made available; equipment in GSA [General Services
Administration] schedules or available through "surplus programs"
should be noted. All equipment marketed by the contractor should
be noted and if same equipment amounts to over 50% of total
equipment and materials costs, then suggested lease-purchase
arrangements should be explained in detail. Estimated delivery
dates for both initiation of ALAC and expansion of program by
a five-fold increase within six months after initiation of first ALAC
should be noted (see part III, below).

6. The Proposal

The proposal to be submitted to the Fiscal Agent, Texarkana,
U. S. A., Dropout Prevention Project should include the above
conditions and provisions, performance requirements, and other
information related to the above in the following format:

Part I

(a) Statement of the problem:

Information based on the contractor's experience in providing
similar instruction to similar target populations should be described, especially if in conflict with existing analyses (see Attach-
ment). The proposal should indicate a clear understanding of the
overall project.

(b) Approach taken:

A detailed description of the approach taken in both reading
and math as well as study skills development should be outlined.
This will include, at the least: 1) student flows; 2) equipment,
materials, and instructional approach to be used, including motivational techniques; 3) conduct of staff training; 4) a management

Exhibit C   179

and logistical plan with implementation of administrative procedures; [and] 5) procedures to insure quality control and effective
on-going evaluation. Any suggested modifications in student selection criteria or other proposed procedures should be justified and
described in detail. Other information which could be utilized by
the Project Manager in planning the size of the ALAC sites, expanding the number of students, etc., should be stated. The contractor should also propose a means for determining when an
enrollee can drop out of the ALAC without penalty to the contractor.

(c) Schedule of performance:

Of particular significance will be initial start-up time required.
Also, the contractor should provide the range of instructional
time per day which is feasible under his instructional program.

(d) Subcontracting:

Specific requirements of all subcontractors will be made explicit; similarly, procedures to insure subcontractor compliance
must be described in detail. A list of contractors with information
similar to that in Part II below should be attached.

(e) Copyrights and patents:

This project is not a developmental effort for the contractor;
however, legal action regarding copyrights or patents might be
expected. The contractor should make his intentions known. Publication right on aspects of the project will normally be at the approval of the Executive Committee.

Part II. Personnel to be used:

The contractor will submit biographical material on all staff professionals to be used in the project. Of particular significance is
the experience of the personnel in dealing with similar projects:
his familiarity with the techniques being proposed, and his ability
to work in an environment such as that in this project. As indicated
earlier, all professional staff will have to be screened and approved
as do existing personnel in the schools.

Part III. Costs and pricing:

Two general cost breakdowns will be submitted:

(a) Instructional costs. Total costs of instruction will be determined on the basis of student achievement per maximum time
period of instruction. The typical student will require 2.5 grade
levels increase in math and reading with appropriate study skills
development. One total should reflect a student population of 150;

another, a population of 400. In order to assist in negotiations or immediate final determination, a matrix, graph, or other summary form of presentation should be included to reflect the differences in costs for students

(1) who have deficiencies in math and/or reading or a combination with different levels of grade deficiency;

(2) who will be enrolled in two subject matters concurrently for removal of varying degrees of deficiency in varying lengths of time;

(3) who have other unique learning characteristics, deficiencies, or situations which will require costs which are unusual.

In those instances where a contractor prefers to propose a cost reimbursable contract, detailed costs will be required on all items. A general fixed fee with incentives contract is highly preferable.

(b) Equipment costs and specs:

The second cost breakdown will include the equipment, instructional programs, tests, and all other material which will be utilized in the instructional process in the ALAC. Specific items with unit as well as total costs will be clearly stated with the names of preferred sales offices where least costs can be obtained. All items listed in GSA schedules or available through "surplus programs" will be noted. Items requiring lengthy delivery time will also be noted with suggestions for reducing that time.

The contractor will also submit a proposed space requirement per optimal student body size (e.g., 30 students per "classroom"). Also included will be refurbishing cost estimates of an existing facility, a recently closed junior high school, which will be the location of one of the ALACs. Refurbishing costs will not be included in the proposal but will serve as a planning guideline and specification for the Fiscal Agent. Facilities for instructional purposes as well as office space will be provided by the Fiscal Agent.

[7.]   *Background*

In December, 1968, the three Texarkana, U. S. A., school districts submitted a preliminary proposal to USOE [United States Office of Education] under Title VIII, Dropout Prevention Amendment. The project proposed to utilize a private contractor who would, on a guaranteed performance basis, remove education deficiencies of potential dropouts. In March, a planning grant was

Exhibit C   181

awarded to the Arkansas School District (designated as Fiscal Agent for the three districts) to develop the operational plan. The Institute for Politics and Planning, under the direction of Charles Blaschke, Manager of Education Programs for the Institute, assisted the school in developing the multi-million dollar, multi-year dropout prevention project, which was submitted on May 5 to USOE.

On May 20, the congressional offices of Mr. Patman and Mr. Pryor were notified that one of the Texas schools and the Arkansas school district were awarded a $270,000 grant (total) to conduct the project. Because the second Texas school district had submitted a freedom of choice desegregation plan, and had therefore been placed on a "deferred status" by HEW, it was not allowed to receive the grant, nor to participate at that time. On May 30, the school board withdrew its freedom of choice plan and immediately became eligible for participation. An additional $250,000 has been requested for their participation; the decision is still pending at this moment [June 10, 1969].[1]

[8.] *The Program*

The five-year Texarkana Dropout Prevention Program will have several major operational components in the initial phases:

(a) A contractor-operated Accelerated Learning Achievement Center (ALAC) which will remove deficiencies in math, reading, and study skills for potential dropouts on a guaranteed performance basis.

(b) Program development for the incorporation of ALAC operations proven effective during Phase I into the 10th–12th grades of the participating schools during Phase II.

(c) Development of programs for those students who would drop out for other than educational reasons: to be initiated in later phases.

The primary long-run goal is to improve the quality of the Texarkana, U. S. A., schools' instructional programs, especially those for low achievers who would normally drop out. The immediate goal is to utilize a private corporation, chosen in competition, to remove the math, reading, and other educational deficiencies of 150-400 students in grades 7-12 in Phase I and 500 students (100

---

1. The Texas request was received too late to qualify for funds.

in grades 7-12, and 400 in grades K-6) in Phase II, thereby preventing them from eventually dropping out; to provide work-study programs in Phase II for 50 students who would drop out for financial reasons; and design a system which will allow for early identification of potential dropouts. The instructional and other programs, developed in initial and later phases, will be integrated into the three school districts' curricula over Phase II, III, and IV. The costs of integrating the self-instructional, individualized, capital-intensive instructional programs proven in the ALAC into the schools and operating them over time will be minimal. The secondary overall goal is to provide a model for other schools in similar situations to follow in preventing dropouts and catalyzing instructional and institutional reform within their schools. Hence, the project has three major components over the five phases: Operational, Developmental, and Demonstrational.

9. Related and ancillary programs

In addition to the funds already awarded to the Fiscal Agent and those requested for expanding the size of the Dropout Prevention Program to include the second Texas school district, ancillary programs which will utilize the facilities of the ALAC and the contractor are being planned for implementation during fiscal year 1970. These programs include:

(a) A special program for 50-100 students who do not qualify for participation in the ALAC because they cannot meet screening standards: most will be designated as disabled learners or mental retardees.

(b) A basic adult education program for 50 adults and recent dropouts who wish to receive a GED [General Education Development certificate].

(c) A special program for about 25 disadvantaged youths who have potential for going to college but are highly deficient in one subject area.

To the greatest extent possible, programs for the above populations will be conducted during "off" hours, in the evenings and on weekends, and will utilize the services of the ALAC contractor. As stated in the proposal, the contractor should describe his interest and capabilities to provide services for these target populations.

Exhibit C   183

10. *Analysis of the situation*

Average achievement scores in Texarkana approximate national norms. However, like most public schools, the districts in Texarkana are not able to provide the necessary assistance to help all of the disadvantaged population.

Over 15% of the school population drops out from the 7th grade on. Many school-age youths are not included in these statistics as they have never enrolled.

In the two participating districts in Texarkana, every year for the past two years, according to official statistics, there have been about 200 actual dropouts, of which a large majority have dropped out for academic deficiencies. An increase of dropouts or "failure to enroll" is expected over the next two or three years as underachieving groups in the Texarkana, Arkansas, school system are integrated with high achievers.

For example, in the Texarkana, Arkansas, school system, there is a difference of median percentile achievement on the Iowa Test of Basic Skills of 60-70 percentiles between school populations slated for racial integration next year. Hence, students far behind in achievement standards will find it extremely difficult to compete with their age peers. Either they will drop out, stay in school but hold back the rest of the class, be set back several grades with younger children (creating social problems), or become "social pushouts."

A similar situation exists in Texarkana, Texas, Independent High School (which will participate [contingent] upon additional funding) which is in its first year as a totally integrated facility. Reading achievement dropped 8.8% after integration. Although few dropouts have been reported, the number of students who did not return to school was not considered. At the 11th grade, 8.2% of the expected students failed to enroll. At the 12th grade, 14% of the expected students failed to enroll. The rate of dropouts can be expected to increase when grades 1-9 are integrated. Critical grade levels appear to be 6-9.

The key to academic deficiencies is [underachievement in] reading, which can be detected in the lower grades. Results of the Iowa Test of Basic Skills indicate that the disadvantaged students start reading at near grade level, then fall further and further behind, while non-disadvantaged students start above grade level and stay there.

Students who have difficulty with reading and other language skills also have difficulty with other courses. Of students failing more than one course at the senior high school level in Liberty-Eylau [the participating district in Texas],62% are failing English and one or more other courses. Conversely, of those students failing only one course, 16% are failing English. Failure in English, therefore, is highly correlated with failure in other subjects.

Failure in English and math are linked. Roughly 25% of those multiple failures failing English are also failing a math course, at grades 10–12. Failures in math and science are linked. Roughly 25% of those multiple failures failing a math course are also failing a science course.

Aside from reading and math deficiencies, all the students participating in the ALAC will require some study skills development. At the third grade level, for example, in the Texarkana, Arkansas, school district, the average student scored at the 70th percentile in work study skills whereas at the ninth grade, his score is approximately 30. This percentile drop is greater than any other as tested on the ITBS.

Additional information plus a detailed analysis will be presented at the bidders' conference [held on June 26, 1969] and/or will be made available upon request to contractors who intend to bid.

11. *Target population*

Students in ALAC will have the following general characteristics:
1. Two to three grade levels behind highest achievers in Texarkana in all areas;
2. Highly deficient in math and reading;
3. Average or above average intelligence;
4. Highly deficient in work-study skills;
5. Highly deficient in communications skills;
6. Low in motivation/job aspiration;
7. Failing in math or English;
8. From low-income family;
9. From poorly-educated family;
10. Achieving below potential.

Exhibit D

Addendum to the Dropout
Prevention Proposal

ADDENDUM TO DROPOUT PREVENTION PROPOSAL,

Sent by Texarkana to U.S. Office of Education, July 1, 1969

Part I: Operational Plan for Accelerated Learning Achievement Center

The purpose of this addendum is two-fold: (1) to provide a brief, concise statement of the goals and operations of Phase I, based on the reduced budget level imposed on the two participating school districts in the Texarkana Dropout Program; (2) to clarify questions raised during the review process of the formal application.

It was understood by all parties concerned that the participation of Texas Independent School District was dependent on the resolution of its HEW desegregation compliance which was in question until May 30, when by public referendum it withdrew its freedom of choice plan. Hopefully the district's desegregation plan will soon receive HEW approval and then they will be reinstated in this project.[1] It will participate with the other two school districts, if an appropriate level of funding is authorized.

1. GENERAL AND SPECIFIC OBJECTIVES OF THE COMPONENT

The purpose of the Accelerated Learning Achievement Center (ALAC) is to reduce the educational deficiencies of those students, grades 7-12, who would normally drop out of school for this reason. The ALAC will also provide a unique testbed for demonstrating the efficiency and effectiveness of various reading and math instructional programs as well as communications and study skills development programs for this target population. For many reasons, described later, the use of the Center also provides the opportunity for determining the demonstration value of experimental approaches and for maximizing the demonstration effect for replication purposes, locally and otherwise. Based upon irrefutable demonstration, the Center's programs, after careful program development and planning, will be incorporated into the participating school districts' programs. Hence, the objectives of this component are operational, developmental, and demonstrational.

   A. Operational Objectives
      (1) To increase the levels of academic achievement of 150 potential dropouts by 2.5 grade levels in the typical case in math and in reading in grades 7-12. Based on previous analysis, 80% of those potential dropouts should remain in school rather than drop out after [completing] the program and [reentering] school full time. A combination of pre- and post-tests, including Iowa Basic Skills Tests (see RFP),

---

1. Their plan was received by HEW too late to qualify for funds.

187

plus additional tests as required will be used.

(2) To remove deficiencies in study and communications skills so that the 150 participating students can re-enter school full time with a low probability·of dropping out due to these deficiencies. Students in Washington Junior High School at the 9th grade were 54 percentile points lower than those 9th graders at Jefferson Junior High School in work study skills. Individual programs will be tailored according to individual needs.

(3) To train 20 junior and senior high school teachers and administrators who will be working as part-time consultants for the ALAC contractor. They will become familiar with and capable of utilizing in their school classrooms in Phase II the instructional programs developed, tested, and demonstrated in the Center during Phase I. The training will be mostly "OJT" [on-the-job training] in the sense that the teachers will be involved in curricula modification, diagnostic testing, and evaluation conducted at the Center rather than formal workshops. Moreover, an additional number of parents and paraprofessionals (15-20) will be hired and trained by the contractor to be used as aides in the ALAC (e.g., to operate and maintain audio-visual equipment, to assist the classroom monitor, etc.)

B. Research and Development Objectives

(1) To develop a general model which will:
   (a) predict the probability of homogeneous groups of students, in grades 7–12, dropping out for academic reasons;
   (b) project existing educational deficiencies inherent in school programs;
   (c) prescribe an instructional program which will most efficiently and effectively remove these deficiencies.

(2) To analyze the relationship between student educational deficiencies in [grades] K-6 and the probability of dropping out at the junior high and above levels. A tentative model will be developed which will:
   (a) allow for early detection of potential dropouts;
   (b) provide insight into the specific factors which contribute directly to low education achievement;
   (c) provide the basis for student selection criteria, determining the nature and extent of the deficiency and indicating the instructional approaches to be developed and tested in Phase II.

(3) To determine the specific costs and instructional time required for grade levels of achievement of groups of students with similar learning characteristics and profiles. These projections will be used by the local school and the Project Manager in planning for Phase II ALAC operations as well as integrating curricula into the local schools, which is the overall most important objective requiring most careful planning during the conduct of Phase I. The operating costs of the

newly-incorporated curricula (grades 10-12) during Phase II will have to be minimal in order that the schools will be able to absorb these costs within existing budgets. It will also provide the basis for similar schools to adopt the contractor-operated approach for instructional reform in their particular schools.

C. Demonstration Objectives
    (1) To demonstrate to the local community, school officials, teachers, board members, and appropriate state and federal officials, that the education process, in part if not in whole, is capable of being managed, and, specifically:
        (a) that quality control in math and reading can be introduced at a 90% accuracy level of prediction;
        (b) that diagnostic tests and institutional approaches based on behavioral psychology and educational technology do allow for predictability of student achievement per maximum time period for students with different learning characteristics;
        (c) that criteria for measuring student achievement in math and reading exists and can be used effectively and objectively;
        (d) that the instructional costs and time savings of math and reading achievement can be reduced by as much as 50% through the use of modern instructional and management techniques.
    (2) To demonstrate to state and local officials that performance contracting and the use of a separately-managed but local school-controlled center is the most effective demonstrational model for:
        (a) experimenting seriously on the local school level while minimizing local political problems;
        (b) gathering hard data in terms of costs/achievement/time/student in order to justify capital outlays, administrative costs of change, and other implementation costs to local taxpayers, school boards, and others;
        (c) removing the NIH (not-invented-here) factor in order to get school officials and teacher acceptance;
        (d) providing a "credible" experiment whose results and approach have greatest likelihood of being adopted by the schools across the country.
    (3) To demonstrate to state and federal officials that the contractor-operated approach is the most effective and least disruptive means for:
        (a) integrating school systems where large educational achievement differences exist between Negro and other minority-group youths and [their] white counterparts by national standardized tests;
        (b) acclimating and training teachers for newly-integrated classes;
        (c) providing true and compensatory education and up-grading for those who need it;

(d) gaining local political and community support for program effectiveness and educational improvement.

2. GENERAL PROCEDURES FOR ATTAINING PROGRAM OBJECTIVES

Philosophically, this component utilizes a unique management approach. The operational component, the ALAC, will use performance contracting, i.e., the contractor will be paid on the basis of how efficiently the student learns. We estimate that one grade level [increase] in math and reading can be guaranteed in not more than 200 hours for not more than $300. Although private firms or groups have been involved in providing education and training services for public agencies (e.g., Job Corps, contracts with parents, etc.), in no instance has a contractor been contracted with by a local school system to provide these instructional services on a learning achievement guaranteed-performance basis.

Because of the acute nature of the dropout problem projected over the next two or so years in Texarkana, U. S. A., and the commitment of the participating school districts to seek every possible feasible solution to their problem (which is also a general regional and national problem), the school districts have accepted the responsibilities of the innovator by conducting this experimental project.

First, this is an experimental project. Hence, the participating school districts have chosen to specify the performance specifications in such a way that the contractor has maximum freedom to achieve the goals (i.e., student learning) and incentives for conducting the job most efficiently without prescribing "how" to proceed.

Second, as the management plan indicates, this concept [will utilize] . . . an outside Managment Support Group to assist and work directly with the Project Manager. The project manager and the Management Support Group will be chosen by the local participating schools, i.e., the Executive Committee. The Management Support group will be responsible to the Project Manager.

Last, the approach taken here to maximize the demonstration effect appears to be unique in promoting the adoption of new instructional methods and catalyzing the institutional improvement of schools.

The school will be involved from the start and contractually will control the operations of the ALAC. Teachers and principals will be utilized as consultants by the contractor, who will also hire and train 20 paraprofessionals. The school will actually purchase all non-expendable equipment, teaching machines, etc., used in the Center (based on the contractor's specifications) and in turn will rent the equipment (e.g., teaching machines, etc.) to the contractor during the period of performance. This will provide additional leverage and bargaining positions for acquiring instructional materials, software, etc., at lowest cost, from contractors or manufacturers. The NIH (not-invented-here) factor will be minimized; teachers' acceptance and capabilities will be expanded; and equipment will be owned by the schools for implementation in Phase II. Since equipment and materials will be purchased by the Fiscal Agent, the criteria of distributing curricula, equipment, etc., to each of the schools in Phases II, III, and IV, will be based on the following: a) extent of the material; b) availability of existing equipment and material; and c) student population.

Also, most exemplary or model programs were not credible to the community and school officials due to the use of expensive research, development, and consultant personnel, the availability of a unique nearby university capability which had few national counterparts, or the high cost of operating the program beyond pilot stage. This project will be credible in the sense that the Center's operations will be similar in concept to a classroom "environment"; the instructional approach which will be utilized will incur minimal operating costs upon implementation into the school as specified in the RFP; local teachers will become familiar with ALAC techniques and will be trained during the time they serve as consultants to the ALAC; and the results of the program will speak for themselves, thereby minimizing arguments regarding subjectivity in the evaluation.

In short, based on the above philosophy and implementation procedures to follow, the assurances of a success are inherent in the following:

1. Incentives for efficiency provided to the contractor;
2. Management support to insure quality control and effective project management;
3. Use of instructional program components (e.g., math program, audiovisual equipment) which have worked elsewhere with not too dissimilar populations;
4. Initial and continuous program planning to predict future problems and opportunities and to insure effective implementation into the schools; and
5. Credible and effective demonstration effects, with procedures for local and national dissemination.

[The remainder of Part I of this Addendum deals with facilities, equipment, and material, and with staffing and personnel.]

Part II: Response to Questions Raised [by U.S. Office of Education]

1. What will be the racial composition of the participants in the ALAC?

Students who will participate part-time at the ALAC while enrolled in the participating school districts at their normal grade level will be chosen on the basis of math, reading, and directly related educational deficiencies which would cause them to drop out of school. Based on the analysis conducted during the planning period, it is estimated that both white and black students will participate in this center's operation and will be drawn from both the Model City as well as non-Model City neighborhoods, as well as the rural areas on both the Texas and Arkansas sides. As stated in the formal application, with the pending integration in September 1969 of the Arkansas School District (where the median difference at the ninth grade between the previous all-black and all-white schools is about 70 percentiles), highest priority will be given to those students who will not be able to compete educationally at the grade level in which they will be enrolled because of two or three years' deficiencies in math and reading. While each of these students will be enrolled in the previously all-white school and will be participating in curricular as well as extra-curricular functions within that school, they will be receiving compensatory education three or four hours per day until their deficiencies are removed. And in no case will this time be longer than the normal school year. This program will not, under any condition, be an "all-black" or "all-white" program.

The selection criteria indicated in the attached RFP and in the formal application (Section D) will be refined during the initial three months and a tentative list of students based on their needs will be provided by the two school superintendents (plus the Texas Independent School Superintendent pending participation approval) for final approval. The advice of knowledgeable teachers, principals, the students' parents, and other school officials will be sought.

2. Why are the overall costs per student participation relatively high?

As the formal application stated very explicitly, there are three objectives: a) operational; b) developmental; c) demonstrational. The single most important objective of the multi-year program is to improve the overall quality of instruction throughout the participating schools. The ALAC, while operational, should be conceived as a demonstration mechanism which will catalyze in a most non-disruptive and effective manner curricula improvement within the schools. Once the ALAC becomes operational, the major management function will be to plan for the effective implementation of those portions of ALAC operations and curricula into the school system based upon irrefutable demonstration of performance increases and/or cost reductions. In order to determine the operating cost for this massive undertaking, the most definitive program budgeting and planning must occur prior to and concurrent with the operations of the ALAC. It is also essential that both pre-tests and post-tests are administered in the most objective manner. Costs cannot be considered without regard to the performance achieved. The relevant cost factor is cost-unit achievement rather than cost-student, a conceptual inadequacy of most educators reflected in part by the manner in which the question was raised. Even if the total program was considered operational, given that most students will require three grade-level increases, the cost-grade-level increase would be comparable to those of most schools. Every effort, as indicated in the RFP, will be made to utilize those instructional programs in the ALAC which can be implemented into the schools at minimal operating cost over time. In Phase II adequate acquisition of equipment and other non-expendable items which will have been proven in the ALAC will be made. During Phase I a cadre of trained teachers and administrators will have been created in order to insure that all equipment, instructional programs, and other materials will be utilized effectively.

3. To what extent will parents from the target area be involved?

In order to assure the maximum involvement of target area parents, a Parent Advisory Group will be established. During the first year the involvement will be focused toward very specific program concerns. During the second year the nature of the involvement will be an integral part of the evolving elements of the program. These programs which will evolve from and will have been planned during Phase I will include the following with minor modifications but not to exclude others which the parents or community would give high priority: a) Saturday program where parents and students receive instruction; b) parent education for early childhood development; c) parent participation in intensive counseling programs; d) planning for programs to be conducted in Phase III.

Exhibit E

Portions of the Proposal by Dorsett
Educational Systems, Inc., to
the Texarkana Schools

PORTIONS OF PROPOSAL BY DORSETT EDUCATIONAL SYSTEMS, INC., TO THE TEXARKANA SCHOOLS

[Introductory portion omitted.]

I. STUDENT FLOW

A. Overall

One of the important ways in which our approach differs from that outlined in the Request for Proposal is in the area of geography and logistics. Precisely because the system we are proposing is largely self-instructional, and because the equipment we are proposing is both portable and inexpensive, we see no necessary reason for transporting all students to one location. . . .

For a wide variety of reasons, primarily economic and social, we would much prefer to locate decentralized branches of the Rapid Learning Center at or in the schools they will serve.

On economic grounds, the merits are obvious. No addition to our staff will be necessary, since six persons will be required either way for the 150 student level and little extra instructional materials or equipment will be necessary; and our basic cost structure for grade-level achievement will remain unchanged. But since we will not be wasting up to one hour of the student's time per day in travel and administration, this hour will be available for additional instruction either in the school setting or in the RLC. It should be noted that this cost-benefit will not be passed along to the contractor, since we will be paid on the basis of clock-time in the RLC, not on calendar-time. But it will work to the benefit of the schools, since more students can be handled per unit time, and thus the fixed costs of operating the RLC will be spread over perhaps a third more students than would otherwise be anticipated.

On social grounds, it seems obvious that the students' self-perception, as well as their perception of the project, would be improved by eliminating the somewhat degrading element of bussing. It is our firm intention to make the RLC concept so attractive, environmentally and educationally, that our students and their peers will look upon attendance as a privilege rather than a stigma. The removal of the bussing interlude will also eliminate one unnecessary potential discipline problem. Further, it will eliminate one possible source of concern within the community.

And finally, it will make for a more meaningful experimental design and model for replication in other communities which will often not have an empty school building available to them. . . .

One of the features of the Centers will be carpeting. It is Dorsett's experience that not only will floor maintenance be reduced, but student behavioral level will be substantially affected by the appearance, resilience, and acoustically quieting effects of carpeting. Adequate reserves will be established for maintenance due to wear and damage due to accidents or vandalism. Another feature of the Center may be the installation of FM stereo receivers which could be tuned to the Texarkana FM station at most times during the school day. In this context, it should be remembered that study will be completely individualized, with permanently assigned headsets, and that lectures and group discussions will be rare, small, and used as reinforcement contingencies or breaks. Obviously, any procedure which depends primarily upon the special personal skill of unique imported professionals is not one which can be rapidly expanded and widely disseminated.

If the utilization of centrally-located space within each school proves to be impracticable, we would then propose the use of prefabricated steel classrooms or wheeled mobile classrooms adjacent to each of the four schools, to be installed at the contractor's expense if necessary. . . .

We would like to assure the project management that we do not think the student's environment is a trivial consideration. Time after time, one or another of our learning centers has found that a given learning task takes $2\frac{1}{2}$ to 3 times as long when performed in a typical public school environment as it does in our facilities. We feel that this is at least partially attributable to the businesslike atmosphere induced by consistently applied contingency management schedules. We work consciously at exhibiting our seriousness of purpose, and when the student perceives that we are actually on his side, he supports and works at that purpose. Accordingly, we will do everything within reason to make the transition from routine school activities to the RLC a "through the looking-glass" type experience, whereby the student will leave behind avoidance behaviors, such as how-not-to study and how-to-play the game. To this end we will attire our staff distinctively, for example in blazers of a particular color. We will also want to insulate our students as completely as possible from routine school activities while they are in the RLC; in order to help enforce this insulation, we will propose that any time one of our students is called out of the RLC for any reason, that no time be charged against our accounting for that student for that full day. Finally, we will want the privilege of dismissing students from the program if and as they disrupt our controlled environment. We do not, by the way, consider the last to be a serious problem quantitatively, based on our previous experience with similar populations.

B. Student Flow Within the Center

1. Orientation Period

It is critically important that a student's first contact with the center be non-threatening and non-aversive. To this end, there will be no testing during his first week of attendance. Instead, cassette tape players will be made available the first day, and each student will listen to a recorded presentation of the purpose and philosophy of the Rapid Learning Center. During the remaining four days of the week he will be encouraged to familiarize himself with the self-instructional equipment, including the Dorsett M86, to select filmstrips that interest him for viewing, to look at single-concept 8mm films, and to browse in the available free-reading material. The only exception to the no-testing rule during the first week will be administration of a 5-minute "fun-and-games" reading quiz on Friday. This instrument, the Ohio Literacy Quiz, has been found in our research to have a high correlation with lengthier and more tedious reading measures.

The results of these quizzes will be analyzed over the weekend to enable our Rapid Learning Center managers to obtain a first approximation of optimum entry level for each individual.

It is anticipated that many, if not most, of our students will be reading below the 7th grade level. Although our overall approach will be heavily audio-visual in nature, thus minimizing the effect of initial reading problems, it is of course obvious that the production of reading achievement is critical to the success of the project, and this area will receive first attention in the Center.

2. Basic Level

As discussed previously we will initially also utilize the Job Corps Reading System, including programed instruction booklets, available from the General Services Administration, for our basic reading program. Therefore, the first event of the second week in the center will be the administration of the appropriate screening instrument. Based on these results, each individual will be entered at the appropriate level of the Reading System. . . . As students complete the Job Corps reading sequence or their initial screening tests indicate no need for it, they will be branched to more advanced reading materials, both programed instruction and audio-visual. Because of the importance of reading skills to other subject-matter, including arithmetic reasoning ("word-problems"), we will use both of the two study-hours in the RLC for reading instruction until the student has demonstrated a minimum of 7th grade achievement. At this time, the second hour of each study period will be converted to math instruction.

Here again, the Job Corps system will be used initially. . . .

3. Progress Checks

Progress checks will be given at frequent intervals, perhaps two or three per week per subject. Frequent progress checks are important when administering programed instruction materials, since some students will tend to try to go through the materials too fast, and will simply turn pages to "get through the book." This behavior will be recognized through observing low scores on progress checks. Others will try too hard to get every step exactly correct and will often go through a lesson two or more times in an attempt to get the best possible scores on post-tests. A large deviation from the mean time necessary to complete a lesson will pinpoint this problem. The self-pacing nature of the programed instructional materials to be used will virtually guarantee that the students will be scattered throughout the course material at all times, and that progress checks will therefore be taken at random and unpredictable times. Since we consider feedback from these progress checks to be a vital part of learning efficiency, we intend to score them immediately and use the results to assign new course material.

Without the use of some sort of scoring device, this would obviously require a great deal of the center manager's time, and would tend to shift the overall project in the direction of a labor-intensive system.

Our solution to this problem will be the use of the Dorsett Telescholar, a small test-scoring device which produces a visible record of students' answers in an IBM port-a-punch card which can be quickly evaluated visually by the instructor for diagnostic purposes. The card is also available for transmittal to the central RLC for later use in the intended item analysis, which will be used to pinpoint weaknesses in the overall system for future refinement and upgrading.

4. Intermediate and Advanced Levels

As students complete the Job Corps reading and math systems, or as their screening tests show no need for it, they will be given more advanced diagnostic instruments, and directed to intermediate or advanced levels. The instruments presently contemplated for this purpose are the SRA Basic Skills in Arithmetic and SRA Reading Record.

The primary instructional media at the intermediate and advanced levels will be audio-visual teaching machines. At the intermediate level, most of the work will be in the area of number facts and vocabulary drill and review. At the advanced level, we will use a recently-produced "Trouble-shooting Math, Grades 7-12" program presented on the Dorsett M86 machine. This program was originally developed for Job Corps needs in a paper-and-pencil programed instruction format.

It would, by the way, be an error to attempt to correlate too closely the study times and costs of isolated uncontrolled anecdotal successes, as in the Job Corps, reformatory schools, or private tutor centers, with the proposed Texarkana program. Where student selections from the entire population having educational deficiencies which are negatively skewed, as at Texarkana, are compared with scattered programs with special selection and motivation providing highly positively skewed groups, there may be an unfavorable difference in study time for given achievement.

At the advanced level we will also select and encourage the individual student to select from a large library of 35mm educational filmstrips in the fields of mathematics and language arts. . . .

5. Graduate Level

Upon completion of the advanced level, defined tentatively as two grade levels [of] achievement in both reading and math, an evaluation will be made of the student's progress to date and, at his option, and with the recommendation of the RLC manager and approval of the Project Manager, he may stay in the RLC program at the graduate level. It is at this level that we feel we are most likely to realize the essential purpose of dropout prevention. We could offer additional reading and math instruction for this higher-achieving student, as well as additional subject matter in other areas designed to maximize the chances of continued success in school, graduation, and a subsequent role as a useful member of society.

Some of the areas proposed to be covered in the Rapid Learning Centers in addition to reading and mathematics include:

1. Study Skills
2. Communications Skills
3. World of Work
4. Career Counselling
5. Dress, Comportment, Personal Appearance. . . .

It will be Dorsett's intention to operate the Centers at or near their effective capacity as soon as they are in efficient operation, which should be within 60 days from the beginning of school. It is hoped and expected that educational deficiencies can be overcome rapidly. It is proposed that in the event the 150 students (or 400) expected to be assigned during Phase I have all been assigned to the Centers and in part de-assigned due to completion of work and excess facilities exist and excess funds from the grants remain, additional students over this number will be assigned and payments made therefore until the available funds have been fully employed. . . .

II. INDIVIDUALIZED AUDIO-VISUAL INSTRUCTION

Few would argue with the suggestion that, all other things being equal, audio-visual instruction should be used whenever possible with disadvantaged populations since these groups typically exhibit both reading disability and reading disinclination.

There is also a considerable body of educational research indicating that students learn more from an audio-visual presentation when some sort of active response is required.[1] And, there is little doubt regarding the effectiveness of immediate and automatic reinforcement of correct answers in any sort of instructional sequence.[2]

It is difficult for us to over-emphasize the importance which we attach to the fact that we are proposing the use of an instructional system that capitalizes on just these techniques, our Dorsett M86 audio-visual teaching machine. Of our own knowledge, this is the only comparable device on the market today that is both in production and inexpensive enough to be used in sufficient quantity to carry much of the instructional burden, as distinguished from a laboratory model or curiosity item.

As noted earlier, we expect to use this machine as the primary source of instruction at the intermediate and advanced levels, and if permission can be obtained to convert Job Corps reading and math programs to this format, at the basic level as well.

Add to this the versatility of also being able to use the same device to individualize the instructional use of hundreds of existing educational filmstrips, and we submit that we will bring to the Texarkana

1. A. A. Lumsdaine and A. I. Gladstone, "Overt Practice and A-V Embellishments," Learning From Films, ed. Mark A. May and A. A. Lumsdaine (New Haven: Yale University Press, 1958.)

2. J. G. Holland, Teaching Machines and Programed Learning, II, ed. A. A. Lumsdaine and R. Glaser (Washington, D.C.: National Education Association, 1965), pp. 66-117.

project an instructional system unavailable from any other source, and one which will help us immeasurably in guaranteeing the achievement of the goals cited in the Request for Proposal. . . .

III. MOTIVATIONAL TECHNIQUES

A. Contingency Management

An important factor in the success of EVCO/Dorsett's learning centers and in the educational research and development performed by EVCO for various government agencies has been the systematic application of the motivational techniques of "contingency management." . . .

The stimulus for the refinement of contingency management was, quite basically, the difficulty of motivating students to complete PI [programmed instruction] sequences. . . . To considerably oversimplify, it was found that a great many activities could be identified which the student would prefer to engage in [rather] than going through a PI sequence. These activities, called high-probability behaviors, can be specified by observing students, asking them, or sometimes prompting them through the use of a "reinforcement memo." Once an appropriate high-probability behavior is identified, it can be used to reinforce the lower probability behavior of attending to an instructional unit.

This system sounds deceptively simple. Many will say that this is how they've always managed behavior. But the key is to let the student himself identify the desired high-probability behavior, and then to make a "performance contract," either written or verbalized, in which the student agrees to perform a certain amount of low-probability behavior in return for the consideration of being permitted to engage in a higher-probability behavior for a specified period of time. These techniques, when applied systematically and consistently, have produced particularly dramatic results with disadvantaged populations. . . .

Apropos of motivation in the public school setting, Professor [B. F.] Skinner has written, "A child will spend hours absorbed in play or in watching movies or television who cannot sit still in school for more than a few minutes before escape becomes too strong to be denied. One of the easiest forms of escape is simply to forget all one has learned, and no one has discovered a form of control to prevent this ultimate break for freedom." . . .

B. Reward System

A distinction should be made between contingency management and a reward system. The latter is just what it implies, a system of

rewarding achievement, not simply for performing a given behavior. In the Texarkana project, we will provide two different reward systems, one for achievement on unit tests, progress checks,
and the like, and another for the basic achievement desired, i.e., a
grade-level increase.

1. Unit Achievement

For this purpose we plan to obtain tokens indicating learning
achievement. These tokens could come in two denominations
(10-unit and 50-unit) and might be convertable to [trading]
stamps. The reward system will be designed so that even a
minimally-achieving student could fill a book very early in the
program and so that a maximum monetary value of $3.00 would
not be exceeded per grade level. (For additional background on
motivational systems of this nature, the reader is referred to
Allyon's book, Token Economies, Appleton-Century Croft, 1969.)

2. Grade-Level Achievement

For a grade-level's achievement gain, we plan to give the student
a transistor radio. Dorsett has sources from which to obtain these
radios for under $3.00. Although we may change our thinking on
this point, we do not now expect to provide alternative "prizes"
for the second or third grade level achieved, assuming that the
students will continue to put forth effort to get another radio for
a parent or friends.

Obviously the implementation of any reward system having
even a nominal monetary equivalent must be cleared with the
Boards of Education through the Representatives or Agent, but
it is hoped that this typical characteristic of private business
operation will be permitted. . . .

4. Parental Involvement

We recognize the difficulty of reaching and getting effective support from the parents of the RLC population. We nevertheless
expect to implement an outreach effort, at least on an experimental basis. If we could influence the parents enough to help
them manage an environment for completing a modest amount
of homework, a great deal would be accomplished. One approach we will try will be to record our message on cassette-type
playback units and send a few home with our students to see
what happens. Another will be to hold an open house for parents
of RLC students periodically, perhaps monthly if attendance

warrants. We will encourage the formation of a Parents' Advisory Group. Other approaches will be tried. . . .

5. Vocational Counseling

The central untested hypothesis of the Texarkana RLC concept is that simple educational achievement will be enough to reduce the dropout problem. We hope in the coming months to demonstrate that this is in fact a workable hypothesis. But we also intend to go one important step further and work with each individual in our student population to help him identify at least one employment goal that is realistic and achievable, and then work with him and show him how it could actually be attained. We feel that we have an obligation to the project, to the schools, to the community, and to the individual, to give him at least one more option than unskilled manual labor at the [nearby government] arsenal. . . .

9. Proposed Method of Cost Reimbursement

We recognize the necessity for keeping the technical and cost proposals separate. We think however, it might aid the reader of the technical proposal if he were aware of the general compensation method we are proposing. Accordingly, we are providing the following proposed guidelines, but have left the figures blank.

Dorsett Educational Systems, Inc. proposes to base its payments on a base fee of _____ for each student-subject-grade level increase at the Centers, times an efficiency factor obtained by dividing nominal hours per grade-level increase (GLI) by the actual hours of study at the Center required per grade level.

For example, if a student achieved one grade-level increase in mathematics in 100 hours of study, a payment of $_____ base fee times _____ nominal hours divided by the 100 hours; or $_____, would be accrued. But if he took only 75 hours, $_____ would be accrued. A similar computation would be required for odd amounts of achievement. If a student advanced 2.2 grade levels in reading achievement in 200 hours of study, Dorsett might accrue:

$$\frac{(2.2 \times \$\quad)(2.2 \times \quad \text{hrs.})}{200 \text{ hours}}$$

An alternate linear approximation to the above formula which avoids high payments for exceptionally rapid learning, but causes the contractor to risk getting very little payment even when achievement occurs after long study, would be $_____ per grade increase, less the number of study hours required to achieve each grade. For example, if one grade increase in math were obtained in 100 hours study, an accrual of $_____ minus 100, or $_____, would be made. With either formula, limits might be established for the lowest and highest rate.

Under appropriate circumstances Dorsett will accept payment schedules of either type. . . .

Exhibit F

Contract Between Texarkana and Dorsett
Educational Systems, Inc.

Contract Between Texarkana and
Dorsett Educational Systems, Inc.

PURPOSE

This subcontract is based upon the RFP [Request for Proposal] dated June 10, 1969, issued by the LEA [Local Educational Authority], the proposal submitted by Dorsett, and a mutually agreed upon Letter of Intent [dated September 12, 1969]. It is intended to stipulate the scope of work, responsibilities, and obligations assumed by both parties, but to the extent that further details are required to interpret matters arising under it the above documents are incorporated by reference.

I. Period of Contractual Obligation
   The period of contractual obligation begins September 10, 1969 and extends until June 5, 1970. . . .

II. Previous Obligation
   The grant terms and conditions of [the program grant between Fiscal Agent for the Texarkana School Districts] and the U.S. Office of Education are incorporated herein by reference and made a part of this contract.

III. General Scope of Work Assumed by Dorsett
   Dorsett agrees:
   A. To organize and operate the instructional component of the first phase of the Texarkana Dropout Prevention Program.
   B. To provide instruction in basic reading, math, and study skills to a minimum of 200 students. The study skills may be measured by inference of the achievement in math and reading areas.
   C. To hire and train local personnel, if possible. These people will come from the target area, as paraprofessionals in the operation of the instructional program.

209

D. To utilize at least 20 teachers and administrators from the participating school systems who will work part-time in the instructional program and will facilitate the contemplated transfer of the Dorsett material to the Texarkana Rapid Learning Centers [which had been called "Accelerated Learning Achievement Centers" in the RFP]. Their first-hand knowledge of the nature and extent of academic problems unique to the Texarkana schools will be useful to the contractor.

E. To operate centers at locations mutually agreeable to the parties.

IV. Selection of Students

A. All students who participate in this instructional program will have grade-level deficiencies, in reading and math, of 2.0 or more as determined by the Iowa Test of Basic Skills [ITBS] or the SRA [Science Research Associates Achievement Series] Tests. Further, all of these students will have no less than the minimum intelligence quotient, as determined by [standardized ability tests] . . . of a regularly enrolled student as required by the two school districts, seventy in Texas and seventy-five in Arkansas, by the Project Management Office or its delegated representative.

B. All students who participate in the first phase of this instructional program will come from grades 7-12 in the regular school system.

C. The makeup of the first 200 students will consist of approximately equal numbers of volunteers, students assigned by counselors, and students randomly selected from those with a grade-level deficiency of 2.0 or more.

D. The makeup of any group of students beyond the initial 200 will be similar to that of the first 200, or will have characteristics determined by the LEA and stipulated by the reference material.

V. Testing

A. The entry status for each student will be determined by the most recent test. The Texarkana, Arkansas, school system used ITBS Form 3 and the Liberty Eylau school district used the SRA Achievement Series, Form D. These tests were given the first week of October 1969. In all cases the tests were given on a group basis and the counselors in the individual schools administered the tests. The same conditions will exist for the post-test as was the case in the pre-test.

B. The parties agree that Dorsett will have the option to ask for retesting or adjustment to entry level standing determined by pre-tests where its diagnostic test shows a substantial difference and that the pre-test may have been insensitive to the actual grade-level deficiency when the deficiency is 2.0 grade levels or more. Diagnostic tests given by Dorsett should be administered under conditions similar to that of the initial pre-test. Further, Dorsett will notify the LEA as to what diagnostic test will be used and will allow observation of the testing by the Project Manager or the Internal Evaluator. The negotiation of the interpretation of these tests will be handled by Dorsett's representative and the Project Manager with the help of the Internal Evaluator. Final determination of whether re-test will be given will rest with the Project Manager.

C. Exit-level achievement will be determined by the ITBS or SRA tests administered by a delegate of the LEA.

D. It is the responsibility of the LEA to report in writing the test results for each student to Dorsett. Results of testing conducted by Dorsett will be conveyed to the LEA in the form of written reports to be the basis for each monthly evaluation. While Dorsett may not administer tests comparable to . . . nationally normed [entry or exit] tests, it will continually obtain progress check tests for each subject unit. The number of such tests successfully completed by each assignee and the scores will be included in the Dorsett monthly report.

VI. Attendance of Students

A. Withdrawal from the Dropout Prevention Program may occur under the following circumstances and Dorsett will be paid on the hourly basis.

(1) Students move out of participating school districts.

(2) Student is chronically truant as defined by locally applicable regulations. Regulations [are] that a student be present 50% of any grade-marking period.

(3) Student suffers prolonged period of illness. Same regulations as truancy.

(4) Student is removed from program on the mutual agreement of the LEA and Dorsett. A student will be considered a legitimate withdrawal if he enrolls in the

program, participates for a minimum of ten hours of instruction, and withdraws from the program for any of the above reasons. If the student is in the RLC for less than ten hours, no payment will be made to Dorsett.

B. In the event that a student withdraws from the program, the LEA will, whenever possible or practical, fill the empty slot with another student, no later than 30 days before the termination of the grant: June 5, 1970. Low academic performance will not be considered an adequate reason for withdrawal from the program until the parties to this contract mutually agree.

VII. Cost of Mobile Facilities and Refurbishing

Dorsett will assume the cost of providing one mobile facility during Phase I of this project to be used as an instructional center at the Texarkana, Arkansas, High School. Two of the four or more Rapid Learning Centers operated by Dorsett are to be refurbished rooms in existing schools. Two or more of the Rapid Learning Centers may be operated in mobile classrooms provided by Dorsett and for which a monthly rental allowance of $95.00 per mobile classroom will be paid by the project. At any time during the contract period the LEA may purchase these mobile classrooms at Dorsett's actual cost less accumulated rental payments.

VIII. Method of Cost Reimbursement

A. In consideration for services rendered, Dorsett will be compensated on the basis of actual student successful performance, not to exceed $135,000.00 in total and subject to reduction on failure to obtain achievements or performance.

B. The student performance differential is determined by subtracting the entering grade-level achievement in math and reading from the exit level. Entry status and exit status are based on the SRA and ITBS tests as weighted on a basis to be determined no later than February 1, 1970. This procedure will be applied to all assignees except withdrawals, and a small number of students, assigned by nonrandom procedures, to be mutually agreed [on] by the parties to this contract, for whose learning services Dorsett will be reimbursed at the average hourly rate of other students.

C. Dorsett will be compensated on the basis of obtaining one grade-level increase per subject area in eighty hours of instructional center study for $80.00, or proportionally for each fraction thereof. For students requiring more or less than 80 hours per subject grade-level increase, the payment to Dorsett per subject grade-level increase will vary according to the formula $80.00 × 80 hours divided by actual study hours required per subject grade-level increase. According to this formula, one grade-level increase per subject area in 110 hours of instruction would cost $58.18. Both parties agree that $106.67 for 60 hours represents the upper limit of the cost reimbursement formula and that if over 110 hours of instruction are required, the payment for a grade-level increase will be reduced by $1.00 per hour for every hour over 110. This payment schedule will result in no payment to the contractor if 168 or more hours are required for one grade-level achievement.

D. Monthly progress payments may be made to Dorsett for reimbursement of not more than an estimated 85% of direct and indirect costs incurred by Dorsett for its operations, provided further that the payments do not exceed the estimated accruals to Dorsett for grade-level gains, based on sampling tests or progress check tests, in the professional judgment of the Project Director. It is noted that repeated testing with the same or similar test instruments used for final audit on student disassignment would contaminate the validity of results, so different tests must be used for interim evaluation.

IX. Availability and Cost of Capital Equipment
  A. Dorsett agrees to sell 95 units of the Dorsett M86 Teaching Machines at a unit price of $200.00 for a total of $19,000.00. All equipment will carry standard warranty. In the event that the contractor fails to achieve substantial gains in the program Dorsett will repurchase the equipment at full price.
  B. During the period of this contract, Dorsett is responsible for the full maintenance and upkeep of the Dorsett-manufactured equipment. In accordance to the standard one-year warranty, repairs will be made on a 24-hour basis or another M86 machine will take its place. An adequate amount of supplies and parts for the M86 will be available. The training of local personnel for maintenance of the M86 will also be part of the program.

X. Use of Consultants Listed in the Dorsett Proposal

It is understood that all key consultants or persons of similar status and staff members listed in the Contractor Proposal will be used on a working level, including site visits. Deletion or addition of consultants must be mutually agreed upon by both parties. The LEA must be satisfied as to the active participation of those consultants used by the Contractor. Dr. James L. Evans will be an active and frequent contributor to this program.

XI. Availability of Instructional Materials
   A. Materials to be used in this instructional program will substantially duplicate that listed in the Dorsett Proposal.
   B. Dorsett will provide materials for medium- and high-achieving students and will have such material available at the instructional centers for testing with a sample population no later than April 30, 1970.

XII. Community and Public Relations
   A. The LEA is responsible for informing parents, instructional center employees, and students about testing procedures, scheduling, dismissal, and progress reports.
   B. All official press releases concerning this program should originate from the I FA.

XIII. Review of Contract

The parties agree that from time to time the LEA may review progress on the program and ask for contract amendments if reasonably anticipated progress is not being obtained.

[Remaining sections of the contract were standard provisions which are not peculiar to a performance contract, and which deal, for example, with equal employment opportunity and certification of non-segregated facilities.]

Exhibit G

Agreement Between Texarkana and the Auditor

THE EPIC [Evaluative Programs for Innovative Curriculums] Evaluation Center [of] Tucson, Arizona, agrees to perform the functions and responsibilities of the outside educational accomplishment auditor for the Texarkana Dropout Prevention Program . . . for the consideration of [about $5,200].

The primary responsibilities of the auditor will be to:

a. Verify the results of the project evaluation, and

b. Assess the appropriateness of the evaluation procedures.

1. Services and Products

Services to be provided are:

a. To critique the evaluation plans submitted by the Internal Evaluator for all project components and to make general recommendations regarding their effectiveness.

b. To critique, verify, and make general recommendations with regard to the products and processes of the Internal Evaluator. . . . These will include the following:

    (1) Identification of pertinent variables

    (2) Behavioral objectives

    (3) Adequacy of measuring instruments

    (4) Monitoring systems

    (5) Calendar of events

c. To provide two audit reports to the LEA [Local Educational Authority] in accordance with paragraphs 4 and 6 hereof. These two [interim] reports will be based upon information gathered from project records, interviews with project personnel, and data gathered from specified measuring instruments utilized by the internal evaluator. A minimum of four on-site visits will be made by an EPIC representative and three progress checks will be made to the project director during the time of this contract.

2. Audit Personnel

[Four named members of the EPIC staff will work on the Texarkana audit—one for eleven days and the others for two days each.]

3. Requirements for Space Documents

EPIC has no need for permanent facilities or secretarial assistance within the Dropout Project; however, it is expected that suitable temporary facilities will be available during on-site visitations, and that transportation will be provided during on-site visits between facilities.

EPIC will require the following documents be provided during the initial audit activities:

a. [U.S. Office of Education] guidelines governing the project
b. Complete and corrected copy of the project proposal
c. Copy of pertinent correspondence and publicity releases
d. Copy of all sub-contracts of project
e. Actual budget expenditures
f. Measurement instrument for each stated behavioral objective

4. Schedule of Reports

It is the intent of the EPIC Evaluation Center to review as completely as possible the activities of the Internal Evaluator of the project. The results of these reviews will be presented in two main written reports during the time of this contract: [the first on March 15 and the second on April 1, 1970].

The content and scope of these major audit reports will be entirely dependent upon the written report of the Internal Evaluator for the project.

5. Sampling Techniques

All forms, checklists, and tests used in the project by the Internal Evaluator will be evaluated as to validity and reliability by testing specialists at the EPIC Evaluation Center. The qualifications of test administrators, testing procedures, test scoring, and analysis of results will be verified.

Due to the importance of the achievement test data for use in payment of project funds, all achievement testing techniques and scoring will be spot-checked and the analysis of results will be re-calculated at the Center. These results will be made available to the Project Director and will be included in the Final Audit Report.

6. Audit Reports

EPIC will hold periodic progress checks with the Project Director to verify the reports of the Internal Evaluator. All written reports will go directly to the Project Director. Fifty copies of the Final Audit Report will be delivered to the Project Director.

The Final Audit Report will include verification of all findings and conclusions submitted in writing by the Internal Evaluator and the assessment of the appropriateness of evaluation procedures.

7. Confidentiality

Only those documents outlined in paragraph 3 of this contract will be requested from the project. All information and findings will be held in strictest confidence by EPIC.

Any publicity release must have the approval of the LEA.

[Remaining sections of this agreement deal with the schedule of payments, the incorporation of the grant terms and conditions, and provision for amendment. In addition, the document included three appendices: a "pre-audit checklist," data on personnel, and a "proposed schedule for audit activities." The agreement was signed in early March, 1970.]

HEW REQUEST FOR PROPOSALS FOR DEVELOPING ACCOUNTABILITY MANUALS

[Section I is omitted.]

II. Statement of the Problem

A. Background

Most Federal programs in education support projects . . . are intended to ameliorate and resolve critical problems in the field. If this mission is to be realized, the design, operation, and management of these projects must incorporate specific policies and procedures directed toward the attainment of accountability objectives; not only for the direct effect on critical problem solution, but also for the indirect effect of generation of support for continued efforts in critical problem areas, as well as for the demonstration of techniques with high potential for the renovation and renewal of traditional program areas.

With the passage of the 1967 amendments to the Elementary and Secondary Education Act of 1965, two new Federal programs were established to support projects in the areas of Bilingual Education and Dropout Prevention. At the time that basic program regulations, manuals, and related materials were being prepared, it was decided that these programs provided an appropriate vehicle for a concerted effort to establish accountability principles in the administration of Federally supported projects in elementary and secondary education through a focus upon specific aspects of project design and management.

B. Accountability Focus

The concern for accountability in Federally supported projects focuses upon twelve factors of project design and management, as follows:
[Community involvement, technical assistance, needs assessment, change strategies, management systems, performance objectives, performance budgeting, performance contracting, staff development, comprehensive evaluations, cost

effectiveness, and program auditing are listed and discussed briefly.]

C. Need for Materials

There remain, however, several urgent needs to be met while new projects funded under Titles VII (Bilingual Education Programs) and VIII (Dropout Prevention Projects) of ESEA are still in the beginning phases of implementation. These needs include:

1. A problem analysis and strategy formation conference to review progress to date in the implementation of accountability principles in design and management considerations of Titles VII and VIII program administration, to include a review of the adequacy of the twelve focus factors identified in (B) above.

2. The development of an Accountability Manual for use by appropriate personnel at local and state levels in the implementation of accountability principles in the design, operation, and management of Federally supported projects, as well as those supported from state and local resources.

3. The development of related software for training programs designed to bring about effective use of the Accountability Manual.

4. The conduct of training sessions for designated Office of Education staff members designed to enable these staff members to effectively demonstrate and use the training software in the training of personnel involved or concerned with project development.

III. Scope of Work

Proposals are requested to include necessary activities to encompass the following scope of work and to accomplish the objectives indicated therein:
[Sections A and B discuss arrangements to be made for a conference to review available materials and plan future strategies.]

C. Development of Accountability Manual

The contractor will develop an Accountability Manual for local and state personnel to use in implementing accountability principles in the design, operation, and management of Federally supported projects, or similar projects supported from state and local funds. Primary user groups are seen as LEA [Local Education Authority] proposal writers, LEA project directors, LEA directors of Federal programs, LEA superintendents, and ESEA Federal program coordinators.

Chapters of the Accountability Manual will include an introductory-overview chapter and separate chapters on each of the accountability factors identified in (II.B.) above, as they may be modified in consultation with Office of Education officials following the conference described in (III.B.) above. While manual chapters will form an integral manual as a whole, individual chapters will be written to constitute a free-standing monograph on each of the identified accountability factors.

Content coverage on each accountability topic will include: (1) basic definition of topic concept and explanation of essential terminology; (2) rationale for inclusion of topic in consideration of accountability; (3) discussion of value of consideration of topic concept in project design, operation, and management; (4) identification of essential elements of topic of which project director and other interested personnel should be aware; (5) criteria to enable project personnel to determine adequacy of essential elements as these are incorporated in project design, operation, and management; (6) illustrations or case examples involving essential elements — adequacy criteria relationship, especially pertaining to Bilingual Education and Dropout Prevention programs, which demonstrate basic alternative approaches to problem solution; and (7) an annotated bibilography suggesting further references on the topic for project personnel.

A free-standing Appendix to the Accountability Manual will contain a model project proposal incorporating and illustrating model approaches in each topic area. . . .

[The rest of the document deals with specifications for field testing and scheduling the manual and related equipment.]

Exhibit I

**Request for Proposals for an
Accountability Project
from Dallas, Texas**

REQUEST FOR PROPOSALS FOR AN ACCOUNTABILITY PROJECT FROM DALLAS, TEXAS

[Part 1 deals with general relations with the contractor.]

2. Performance Requirements of Anticipated Activities: Management Support Group

a. *Design, develop and implement a management information system which will:*

    (1) Report student progress toward interim and final performance objectives, by treatment configuration, by school, by contractor (if more than one contractor is involved in instruction) and by individual results, to the following officials for the following general purposes: [lists those who require such data].

    (2) Report actual costs as well as assigned costs of other resources to the Project Manager at predetermined dates to be used for cost effectiveness analysis, sensitivity analyses and trade-off analyses in order to determine the optimal configuration and feasibility of Turnkey operations.

        (a) Develop the relevant procedures, forms, timesheets, etc. for the implementation of the management information system.

        (b) Design and develop a computer-based model for determining the relative cost effectiveness of the nine treatment configurations, the relative cost effectiveness of the three most cost effective configurations in comparison to the Dallas Independent School District's [DISD] counterpart programs, and administrative costs and the projected cost effectiveness associated with performing the Turnkey process when [an] appropriate compatible interface must be assured in terms of data inputs, outputs, and other similar requirements between the model which is to be developed and the existing evaluation design and goal assessment criteria, as modified upon contractor negotiations and by the direction of the Education Audit Group. Refine and/or modify extant or newly developed procedures which will be used by the Project Management Office during the administration of the project. . . .

(e) Conduct the necessary cost effectiveness analyses as indicated in activities (1) and (2) above with recommendations presented to the Dallas Independent School District Project Management Office, other school officials, and the Dallas Independent School District Board of Education:

[1] Relative cost effectiveness in terms of cost per level of increase, by unit of instructional time and/or student learning characteristics.

[2] The actual costs and cost of administrative and other changes to implement the three most cost effective treatment configurations into the Dallas Independent School District counterpart program in the Project senior high schools, beginning with the ninth grade at the end of Year 1 of the Project.

[3] The relative levels of guarantee which the contractor will make if the program is adopted by DISD, conditional upon changes in administrative procedures and cost outlays to be made by DISD to be presented in terms of alternative costs and benefits to relevant decision makers.

3. Statement of Anticipated Activities: Education Audit Group

The Education Audit Group will serve in a staff capacity to the Project Manager's Office during the first year of the Guaranteed Student Achievement Project . . .

The Education Audit Group will advise, and provide technical assistance to, the Project Manager in the general areas of process, product, and management evaluation as applied to the Guaranteed Student Achievement Project. In the fulfillment of these duties, the Education Audit Group will be required to perform the following services in accordance with specified product and delivery dates as estimated below, but to be firmly established by the time of contract signing.

a. *To review, modify and certify the Project's goals and evaluation design.* The Auditor will examine the design, the proposed instruments, the data collection procedures, the statistical treat-

Exhibit I 231

ments, and the Project's goals and objectives. He will make recommendations as to the internal logic of the design, the validity and reliability of the instruments, and the administrative feasibility of the total evaluation process. He will assist the Project Manager in making recommended changes and will certify the final product.

b. *To advise the Dallas Independent School District during contract negotiations with the contractors who are offering instructional goods and services which will be utilized in the Project.* Such advice will pertain to the merits and weaknesses of each bidders' program(s), interim and final objectives, method of performance, measurement, instrumentation and cost-reimbursement proposals.

c. *To review, modify, implement and monitor the Dallas Independent School District's proposal evaluation process.* The Auditor will establish criteria that expand upon, but do not basically change, the criteria and weighings stipulated in the request for proposals provided potential bidders. The objectives of the Auditor's proposal evaluation process will facilitate neutrality, objectivity and ease in the review.

d. *To develop an audit design.* The Auditor will submit for the Project Manager's approval an audit design for Year 1 of the Project. The design proposal, with supporting documentation, instrumentation and rationale, will be directed at the assessment procedures and instructional processes and products.

e. *To implement the audit design.* The Auditor will be responsible for instrument development and validation, determining and certifying testing conditions, receipt of data from the DISD testers, statistical analysis of the data, formulations of conclusions, and presentation to the appropriate decision makers. . . .

f. *To supervise and certify all measurements, tests and other assessments upon which contractor payment is based.* The Auditor will ensure that testing conditions are comparable, that the instruments and their component parts are confidential, and that contractor payment is based solely upon their results, both in the interim performance and final product assessment.

Index

Index

The text of this book is set in Bodoni Book, one of
the family of modern typefaces based on a style
developed by G. Bodoni and introduced in France
shortly before the French Revolution. Composition
was done by Applied Typographic Systems of
Mountain View, California.
This book was printed on Glatfelter Vellum offset paper
by Maple Press of York, Pennsylvania.